The Tax Guardian.com

T0116502

The Tax Guardian.com

Walter F. Picca

iUniverse, Inc.
New York   Bloomington

Copyright © 2009 bt Walter F. Picca

All rights reserved. No part of this book may be used or reproduced by any means, graphic, electronic, or mechanical, including photocopying, recording, taping or by any information storage retrieval system without the written permission of the publisher except in the case of brief quotations embodied in critical articles and reviews.

iUniverse books may be ordered through booksellers or by contacting:

iUniverse
1663 Liberty Drive
Bloomington, IN 47403
www.iuniverse.com
1-800-Authors (1-800-288-4677)

Because of the dynamic nature of the Internet, any Web addresses or links contained in this book may have changed since publication and may no longer be valid. The views expressed in this work are solely those of the author and do not necessarily reflect the views of the publisher, and the publisher hereby disclaims any responsibility for them.

ISBN: 978-1-4401-5441-6 (sc)
ISBN: 978-1-4401-5445-4 (ebook)

Printed in the United States of America

iUniverse rev. date: 07/23/09

Contents

FOREWORD

The some of these postings have been corrected or revised from the original postings.

BLOG POSTINGS
FROM
2/11/08 TO 1/31/09

MODEL INCOME TAX

(revised)

The 10 percent increase of the income tax rate on the third bracket on an income increase of $23,025--and a 2 percent tax rate increase on the top (or sixth) bracket on an income increase of $188,819—in 2008; for example, that is unfair, discriminatory and hits low-income workers the most. There should be at least one bracket of 20 percent between the 15 percent and 25 percent. That would make the graduation of the tax rate more even (or fair). The income tax marginal rates should be based on a linear mathematical formula. For example, a 5 percent increase on the income tax rate on each higher bracket with each successive bracket spread-- increasing 90 percent--would look like this. Beginning with the first (or lowest):

TAX RATES	BRACKETS
5%	$0 to $5,001
10%	$5,001 to $14,501
15%	$14,501 to $32,551
20%	$32,551 to $66,846
25%	$66,846 to $132,006
30%	$132,006 to $255,810
35%	$255,810 to $491,037
40%	$491,037 to $937,968
45%	$937,968 to $1,787,136
50%	$1,787,136 to $3,400,555
55%	$3,400,555 to $6,466,051
60%	$6,466,051 to $12,290,493
65%	$12,290,493 to $23,356,932
70%	$23,356,932 and over

This progressive tax table is non-discriminatory. Now, you ask: why go that high? because, incomes in the US goes that high and much higher. If, you tax the bottom of the income scale—why not the top: that's fair. Like, Ralph Nader says: "I'd really put meat in the progressive taxation." The reason for that: the rich and super rich are under taxed. However, no one tax table fits all situations (or countries). And tax rates should not be fixed, but adjustable with the changing economic conditions. My model tax table is low— compared to some other countries. For example, these are the top marginal tax rate for:

Demark: 63% over 360,000 Danish Krone

Sweden 56% above 374,000 Krone

Netherlands   52% over 53,860 EUR

China 45 % over 360,000 RMB

Australia: 45% over $180,000

Germany 45% over 250,000 EUR

Italy   43% over 100,001 EUR

France 40%   beyond 66,679 EUR

Japan 40% over 18,000,001 Yen

UK   40% over 34,600   British pound, etc.

Note two things: these countries have a higher top income tax rate—and it is levied on a lower level of income or bracket; than, the US. Because, the US budget is super-big and the income range between bottom and top—extremely high: the top income tax rate should be much higher. The income of the top 400 taxpayers—averaged: $263 million in 2006. Ralph Nader says: "The richer people are, the more the percentage you pay." His answer to the question: Why should the rich pay a larger percent of their income than middle-income people? He answers: "It's because their power developed from laws that enriched them."

I would add: the nation's natural resources, the labor of others, and the many services provided by the government, such as: the three branches of government, national defense, healthcare, education, transportation, etc.

In 2005, the US average pay of CEOs to worker was 411:1 in Europe 25:1. Therefore, higher marginal tax rates are justified—to pay for government expenses; but, instead of being raised—they have been lowered.

Grover Cleveland, the 22nd and 24th U.S. president, declared himself in favor of the income tax.

The Sixteenth Amendment gives congress the power to tax income. And, President Woodrow Wilson, who regarded himself--as the personal representative of the people--instituted the graduated federal income tax in the Underwood Tariff (Bill) in 1913, and since, has become a permanent part the US tax code and most industrialized nations of the world.

The Internal Revenue Code of 1954 consisted of 24 income brackets: ranging from 20%

to 91%. Since then, plutocratic-lawmakers have pealed off the top brackets and drastically cut the tax rates.

It is like two armies on the battlefield trying to gain territory on the other--and the rich are winning over the poor. The number of billionaires are rising and those falling below the poverty line. Donald Trump did not make his $2.944 billion estimated wealth in 2006--by labor. It was by investment strategies and (unfair) tax-breaks and cuts.

One: the 1030 Exchange or Starker Exchange: permits the roll over of capital gains of one property into the second: this has a double purpose: it converts a short term capital gain into a long—and permits wealth building without paying taxes. That puts the investor in a better position to purchase a third commercial or residential property, and on and on. The third benefit: depreciation write downs; mostly phantom, shelter property income from state and federal taxation.

How much he paid in personal and corporation income taxes--in his jump of wealth from $500 million in 1990--to $2.944 billion in 200--will tell whether the US legal system and Tax Code is rigged—the same with Warren Buffett. In 2006, he paid 17.7 percent on income of $46 million. One reason for this: Bush lowered the tax on capital gains and dividends to 15%—in 2003.

The NY Times states: "That the rich are getting richer faster, much faster."

Today, the income tax code has six brackets: ranging from 10 to 35 percent. But, we have a growing mammoth National Debt. McCain is proud: he supported the Reagan tax cuts. The reason he did: he is in top 1 percent that owns 42% of financial wealth in 2004. And, that explains why he is a republican—and voted in favor of the 2 year extension of the capital gains and dividend tax cut: 45.3 percent of these tax cuts will go to households with incomes of more than $1 million. Less than 1 percent will go to the bottom 40 percent. Today, the bottom 80%--own only 7% of financial wealth, which includes: corporate stocks. It's an unfair capitalistic system, when some men are multi-billionaires —and others lack basics.

Another big reason: for this wealth and income disparity: the flattening of the income tax by Reagan and Bush on the rich and superrich. Despite--the doubling of their share of total income from 1980—receiving 21.8 percent in 2006: their taxes have been cut roughly in half. That is wrong!

A third reason—for the growing federal deficit: corporations paid over a quarter of the federal expenses in 1950 and a mere 6 percent in 2002-2003. Despite record profits—they pay less taxes. Corporate lobbyists have influenced lawmakers to give corporations tax-breaks—they don't deserve.

Therefore—tax reform is desperately needed. The reason it is not done: plutocrats control the Congress--and the corporate owned mass media has become a launching pad for their opinions and goals.

David Cay Johnson exposes in his book: **FREE LUNCH: how the wealthiest**

Americans enrich themselves at government expense and stick you with the bill—but, it gets no media play—anywhere close to Hollywood celebrities and sport figures. It is ignored (except by PBS).

He states: "Donald Trump benefits from a tax specially levied by the state of New Jersey for the poor. Part of the casino winnings tax in New Jersey is dedicated to help the poor. But $89 million of it is being diverted to subsidize Donald Trump's casino's building retail space."

Bill Moyers asked: "How does that happen?"

David Cay Johnson: "Political connection, the news media not paying enough attention."

Here is another example:

He states "Well, this is one—this is a great irony. George W. Bush owes almost his entire fortune to a tax increase that was funneled into his pocket and into the use of eminent domain laws to essentially legally cheat other people out of their land for less than it was worth to enrich him and his fellow investors."

I am not knocking wealth building: I, just, want it to be fair.

Posted 2/12/08

TAX ISSUES

I recently, read **Pope Benedict XVI** is working on a doctrinal pronouncement that will condemn the use of offshore tax havens as immoral and "socially unjust". Multimillionaire presidential candidate Mitt Romney—did just that as a businessman and claims: it is OK (i.e., tax evasion).

On tax issues: between the two front running presidential candidates: Hillary Clinton is best and John McCain is worst. Here are the reasons:

John McCain is a greedy man—he voted YES—on repealing the Death Tax. This is a goal of the Republican Party. **Warren Buffett says repealing the estate tax or the "death tax" as republican critics call it helps only the rich who don't need it.** He has no credible solution for balancing the budget. The projected deficit for 2009: $408 billion. That is the partial deficit. The total federal deficit will be $100-$200 billion larger. He voted YES on repealing the AMT. It was designed to prevent high-income households from using tax-breaks and deductions to pay little or no income tax. Worst of all, he favors making the Bush tax cuts permanent. According to the Center on Budget and Policy Priorities: **extending the presidents tax cuts and AMT relief would cost $4.4 trillion through 2018.** He wants to cut waste in the government, but that is not enough. He also favors a flatter tax, which favors the wealthy. He is supported by the billionaire Forbes. And, in 2006, he voted NO on $47 billion to strengthen the military and reduce the deficit—by repealing the immoral capital gains and dividends tax cuts. That is enough to justify his imprisonment and torture in Vietnam.

And, most people may not know this: McCain voted YES on requiring a super-majority for raising taxes. That tilts the law-making process in favor of the republican plutocracy. He is a people's traitor.

Hillary Clinton has better judgment. She voted NO—on repealing the Death Tax. It is a fair tax. She is in favor of letting the Bush tax cuts expire. That would help balance the budget. She voted NO on repealing the AMT; although, it has several major flaws: it is better then nothing. And she voted YES on $47 billion to strengthen the military and reduce the deficit by repealing the immoral capital gains and dividend tax cuts. She is a better representative of the people. And, she voted NO on the GOP Tax Plan (i.e., requiring a super-majority to raise taxes).

The Bush-Cheney Administration has defied the will of the people on taxes--and misled them. And, the major TV networks, newspapers and magazines have been co-conspirators (read my book: *Why the Reagan and Bush Tax Cuts are Unfair*): Bush Jr. will go down in history—as the Greatest Creator of Public Debt. And, after six years of consecutive deficits and a projected deficit in 2008 and 2009—he, still refuses to repent. Not a good Christian.

I believe increasing the income tax rates 1 percent (or more) up the ladder, if there is a deficit, and decreasing it 1 percent (or more), if there is surplus—or expand or contract the brackets--is a sound principle. Bush believes a tax cut in favor of the rich is justified for both surpluses and deficits. His main motive: self-enrichment and loyalty to the Republican Party—agenda. He prefers dumping the deficit on future generations, who did not create the deficit.

Posted 2/14/08

HUCKABEE'S FAIR (BAD) TAX

I was amazed by Mike Huckabee's speech on Super Tuesday, he said: "When I get to be president"...."I really do look forward to nailing the 'going out of business' sign on the front door of the IRS."

And there was applause by his supporters.

Actually, his fair tax—would make matters worse. The fair tax—or 23 percent consumption tax—would not possess the benefits of the estate tax, which would be eliminated.

It would eliminate the capital gains tax—which would make those who control the capital—meta-super rich (not the working man, who has little or no money to invest).

It would be a heavier burden on the middle income taxpayer—than, the income tax: the rich would pay less tax.

It would eliminate payroll taxes: that means retirement and Medicare benefits for the retired. Workers would have to pay for these benefits in a plan provided by the private sector: risky, no tax savings.

It would not eliminate the IRS: It would still be necessary to have a federal tax bureau to collect the tax from retailers. Some would cheat.

Cash grants to low income earners—to compensate for the regressive burden of the 23 percent consumption (or federal sales) tax—is crazy. Cash grants—money not earned --would be spent foolishly by many—on alcohol, drugs, etc. And, if billionaire Donald Trump tries to avoid the sales tax—as he says: I am sure most low and middle income taxpayers—would do the same: buy goods on the black market that would crop up—or in Canada or Mexico.

Another problem: by eliminating IRS: how would the government determine—the size of taxpayer cash grants. It could not. People move around, get married, change their names, have children, change their jobs, lose their jobs, get divorced, incomes vary from year to year, people die, etc. Cash grants would cost: $600 to $780 billion a year and climb. There would be a lot of fraud. Much of that money would be wasted--once gone—low-income families would be faced with a 23 federal percent sales tax on goods; plus state sales tax. It would be a disaster.

Corporations would pay no income (or profit) tax.

It eliminates progressive taxation: the gap between the rich and poor—would dramatically—worsen.

It shows the low level of intelligence of his Arkansas supporters--or they don't understand his Fair Tax—or are rich republicans.

Three types of people like Huckabee's Fair Tax: low—income taxpayers who want a yearly cash grant and would buy their goods on the black market or across the border, the rich—who would pay less taxes, and fools. Listen: if, corporations pay no taxes, and the rich pay less, and the poor—get cash grants: the middle-class—will have to make up the difference. Beware of this guitar playing Baptist-preacher from Arkansas. He is a well intending idiot.

RENDER UNTO CESAR, THAT WHICH IS CESAR'S

(revised)

The Tax Foundation estimates 43.4 million filers paid no income tax in 2004: that is not right. The reason: every taxpayer derives some benefits from the federal government. Therefore, there should be a minimum alternative tax: exclusions, credits, deductions, shelters, smart investments, etc.—should not wipe out all debt owed to the government. About 41 percent of filers received benefits from the federal government—and pay no taxes: that is a wrong. You can either clean house on these deductions—or devise a better AMT. To do this: I would impose an alternative minimum tax on AGI or preferably, adjusted net income; because of the growing number of above the line deductions. I would use my model income tax table. I would skip the bottom three brackets and on the fourth: imposed a 5% minimum tax, and I would increase the tax 5% on each higher bracket: 10%, 15%, 20%, etc. After, all data is collected and analyzed: I might decrease (or increase) the minimum alternative tax rate 1% (more or less)—or expand or contract the brackets: from time to time—as economic conditions change. I would make some hardship exceptions, e.g., for natural disasters, etc. I would junk the present skewed and defective AMT. That would make the tax code more fair and simple.

There is a book--titled: How to Pay Zero Taxes: that makes it clear: the tax code needs a thorough overhaul. The author of the book: calls our tax code a "national disgrace." The code tax should be designed to pay for government expenses—and everybody should pay their fair share. And the facts prove: that is not the case. It must be corrected. The number of deductions and schemes are mind-boggling. I did look through them--and found some of them overly generous and frivolous; e.g., organic foods, massages, meat diet, sexual therapy, mortgage interest on a vacation home, etc. Deductions, primarily, should be made for the survival of the individual—or necessities. The numbers of deductions and strategies--makes it impossible for the government to collect enough taxes for outlays. Individual deductions must be balanced against what the government needs to survive—or pay its expenses. Some personal deductions, schemes, exclusions—shortchange the federal government. For example, deductions for state and local taxes: that is going too far: state and local taxes do not pay for federal expenses. This is not double taxation. Besides, tax deductions—there are a growing number of tax credits. Congress sets the marginal tax rates—and then, goes about adding this and that deduction (or credit)—until no tax is paid. That is why the Alternative Minimum Tax is necessary. However, some deductions and credits are justified and have a purpose. For example: deductions for property taxes and interest on a mortgage for a primary residence might be justified—after that it becomes a slippery slope—a second (or vacation) home, a yacht, an airplane, etc. Many of these deductions and tax strategies are designed to avoid taxation—generally, benefiting the rich. Therefore, every deduction, exclusion, and tax shelter should be examined--to determine; if is fair to the individual, the government—and other individuals who must make up the difference. In 2005: 7,386 federal tax returns with AGI of $200,000 or more paid no taxes. There has been a steady increase in the number of cases of individuals with large incomes, that pay little or no taxes—year by year. That tells us: the tax code badly needs reform—and the fact—the US national debt is growing faster than gross national product, since 1980, except for several Clinton years.

Posted 2/24/08

QUOTE

"Large corporations and the wealthy used to pay their fair share. They do not anymore."

— Rockridge Institute

I have often stated—that—and I will give you an example: John Edwards and wife paid 5.1 percent tax on income of $434,000--in 2006. The 2006 lowest tax rate for married—filing jointly: is 10% on income from $1 to $15,100. I do not know what the deductions were: I do believe it was legal. I have gotten some help from Donald Trump, here is what he said concerning the federal deficit (1999): "I say--it is only reasonable to shift the burden to the most able to pay." I agree. His plan: impose a 14.5% tax on individuals and trusts with a net worth over $10 million. This, he says will generate $5.7 trillion to eliminate the deficit. This--I don't agree. In exchange for this: he wants to repeal the estate tax. Not so fast Donald Trump: the estate (or inheritance) tax is an American principle---it is universal and cannot be purchased (or sold).

What I agree with: is a one time tax—on wealth to cut the deficit in half—or one-third—because, for the last 27 years the rich and super rich have been under taxed, because of the Reagan and Bush tax cuts. Donald Trump—you are smart, but you are fired.

Here is a case in point: Ms Heinz Kerry paid in 2003: 15% on $2.2 million in dividends. That is an annual savings of $440,000 until the year 2011—because of the Bush tax cut on dividends. Furthermore, John Kerry and wife paid: 13.4 percent on declared income of $5.5 million. That I believe—is under taxation.

And did some further checking: billionaire Donald Trump paid—as the article reads: a measly $236,000 in taxes in 2002. Ditto.

According to a Forbes report: the richest 400 earned an average of $263 million in 2006 and paid an average tax of 17 percent: that is down from 30 percent in 1995 and 23 percent in 2002. They are earning more and paying less—and the National Debt is going up. That is blatantly wrong.

Posted 2/26/08

TO CALIFORNIA

(revised)

California is facing a $14.5 billion budget deficit in 2009—and Governor Schwarzenegger has proposed--to solve the problem by:

- Making a deal with the Indians to help fill in the budget gap

- Cut 4 billion from children's health care program

- A 10 percent cut in payment to Medi-Cal and education

- Release 30, 000 non-violent prisoners

- Close 48 state parks--and that is just the beginning.

One place--he has not looked: some 52 percent of profitable corporations pay no tax at all--and 1300 California households with over $200,000 of income, who paid no personal income taxes at all. And what is most shocking of all: California has 572,000 millionaires and 98 billionaires and California's six marginal income tax rates are targeted at workers and the middle class.

For 2007, there is a six-bracket rapid progressive tax increase of 9.3 percent on income from $0 to $44,814 and stops. After that, there are no higher marginal tax rates on income that goes into the: millions of dollars. That is not fair. For example, Schwarzenegger's income for 2001-2: topped $57 million. He will pay the same 9.3 percent income tax rate—as those in the sixth bracket—earning: $44,814 and over. And, there is one more disparity: the percentage increase on the third, fourth, and fifth bracket: 2 percent—**here it is:** on the sixth and highest: the percentage increase: 1.3 percent. That is the power of the rich on lawmakers: to reduce or block tax increases on their income and wealth. Schwarzenegger is a rock-hard republican—like, Bush on taxation. He vetoed a bill to merely study the disparities between book income and taxable income reported by corporations. And, he is firm about not raising taxes; particularly on the rich. The average Californian pays enough state taxes—but, not those making over $150,000. Schwarzenegger will not make his tax returns public. He is hiding—this great disparity of income and taxation in California between the middle and the rich.

There is a 1% surtax on incomes of $1,000,000 and over to pay for mental health programs—but, that is not part of the income tax tables.

Posted 2/27/08

CLINTON-OBAMA DEBATE (TEXAS)

(revised)

To the question by CNN's Campbell Brown: how would a President Obama be different than President Clinton in managing the nation's economy.

I was troubled by part of his answer: he said: "Senior citizens making less than $50,000 shouldn't have to pay income on your Social Security." He is wrong and veered off course. This is pandering to get votes. In the first place: less than one-third of current beneficiaries pay tax on benefits. Social Security benefits, generally, are not taxed, unless one has substantial additional income. Senior citizens: do not need more tax-breaks; than, they already have. Once, they retire—they are no longer productive; but, they continue to be an expense to the government—and enjoy the benefits of the government. What is the justification for $50,000 of income tax-free: four times the minimum wage? Obama's proposal, if enacted— would add 7 million more people to the number that the US government supports—that pay no income tax.

Right now—social security benefits; are exempt from taxation, unless a senior citizen's combined income exceeds $25,000 for singles and $32,000 for married couples; then, 50 percent of their benefits are subject to the income tax and 85 percent; if, the combined income exceeds: $34,000 and $44,000. That is reasonable. Plus, they get subsidized housing, meals, transportation, etc. Why should they get a free ride—up to $50,000? That is crazy.

A second thing Obama said: "So I've said that if you are making $75,000 a year or less, I want to give an offset to your payroll tax that will mean $1,000 extra in the pockets of ordinary Americans." This is pandering to a different class of voters. He says: "we pay for these by closing tax loopholes and tax havens that are being manipulated."

What loopholes?—be specific. Are you going to close the loopholes--first—or give the tax breaks—first. That is easier said than done—the congress makes the tax-laws—not the president. He said in the debate: "I want to…."—but at rallies: he says: "I will…."

The needed tax cut—is between the 15 percent and 25 percent bracket and that is not the middle class. And the lowest bracket: should probably be: 5 percent.

The saddest thing about this debate: CNN's Campbell Brown—did not ask one question—on tax issues. This subject is off-limits. It might expose—these massive disparities—in our tax code. She did not pin down what Obama meant: by a $1,000 offset to payroll taxes. I doubt: the listeners knows what he means: whatever it meant: it got an **applause.** What he is proposing is--taking tax-breaks from corporations and giving them to individuals: that does not solve the federal budget deficit. Many people are not paying their fair share—including some at the bottom. There is a difference between what people want and need. What makes these people think—their taxes are too high: they are living beyond their means. What is needed is belt-tightening--instead.

I did not know what the Obama meant: when he said: I want to give a $1,000 offset to your payroll taxes. So, I did some research. Here is what he said back in September of 2007: "I'd reward work by providing an income tax cut up to $500 per person—or $1,000 for each working family—to offset the payroll tax that they're already paying." The payroll tax: should be seen as an annuity--not a tax. It sounds: like he is compensating people for paying the payroll tax. I don't know the details of his plan—but, he did say this: "my proposal would effectively eliminate all income taxes for 10 million working Americans." This—I cannot agree with. I believe every single American should pay some federal tax—on income of $14,350 if, only $500. The cost of his plan: $85 billion.

We already—have the earned income credit—which is an anti-poverty tool for low income singles and families.

Here is the part I agree with: Obama said: "We have to end the Bush cuts to the wealthy…"

On taxes: the difference between Obama and Hillary is very little. Obama has a slightly better voting record: he voted NO--on the extension of the dividend and capital gains tax cuts. But, these two statements: by Barack in the debate—shows he is willing to stoop to pandering—to get votes. I found nothing in Hillary's statement—that I can criticize; except, it was generalizations: no specifics. She said: "Well, I would agree with a lot that Senator Obama said, because it is the Democratic agenda."

THE POLL TAX

You know—I was bothered by Obama's statement: that seem to indicate: he was proud--his plan—would deliver 10 million people from paying the federal income tax. You know that is anti-government, anti-American, and it is anti-Christian--and I say that; because, he claims to be Christian and that is not what Jesus taught. Read Matthew: 22:17-21

And I am also bothered by his words: his deduction—would offset the payroll tax. He seems to interpret the payroll tax—as a government tax—rather than a tax for the individual—that is not brilliant.

The poll tax is a basic principle of government—what it means: everybody that benefits from government—should pay a tax. But, Obama's plan would free 10 million with incomes up to $75,000. That is satanic. That should not be his goal. It should be--to enforce—the poll (or head) tax.

Oliver Wendell Holmes Jr. said: "Taxes is the price of civilization." If, Obama and his 10 million supporters don't like paying taxes: they should go to Darfur and live. There are no taxes and no government.

I wonder if—Obama would like to rephrase what he said—or is he standing firm: what he said is right. I would like an apology.

Do these people receive benefits from the government—and are they able to pay some federal income tax: yes or no?

I am not advocating a Poll Tax—I am advocating the principle of the Poll Tax, which Obama's plan--subverts.

MCCAIN

Senator John McCain is a turncoat on taxes. He voted NO on the 2001 $1.35 trillion and 2003 $330 billion Bush taxes cuts (favoring the rich) and reversed himself—in order to get support to run for president on the republican ticket. They question: his conservatism. He pledges: not to raise taxes. He is not being realistic. Unless taxes are raised: the federal deficit will grow—and that will make things worst for every body. McCain is right on one issue: his determination—to stop pork-barrel legislation. But, that is not enough to balance the budget. Considering the National deficit has been growing at the rate $1.62 billion a day since—September 29, 2006--McCain's pledge--not to raise taxes--make him a pugnacious half-wit. There is no way to reduce the deficit—except by cutting expenses and raising taxes. The fact, he has stated—as the Republican candidate for president: he want to make the Bush tax cuts permanent--makes him—a bad choice. The Independent Ross Perot—back in 1992, told the American people: that the government squandered their money and the $4 trillion debt was so large, it almost defied description, and to reduce it: he proposed: raising the marginal income tax rates of the wealthy. He was right. President Clinton did this. However, after the Bush tax cuts—the deficit climbed from $5.9 trillion to over $9 trillion—in seven years. Robert Reich, the former 22nd Secretary of Labor and now professor at the University of California at Berkeley, states: "Rolling back the Bush tax cuts for the wealthy will yield some $200 billion more. But the new president should not stop there because the only people who have the money necessary to reverse the nation's troubling trends are at the top." This means: making the income tax progressive to the top—opposed by McCain, the republican nominee for president. He believes letting the Bush tax cuts expire—would be a tax increase. The democratic candidates want to end the Bush tax cuts—or increase taxes on the wealthy—they have better judgment—or correct vision.

When Stephanopoulas asked: McCain: "But under **no** circumstances would you increase taxes? He answered: "**no new taxes.**" That is when he made a pack with the devil. He became irrational. He succumbed to party pressure.

However, on earmarks—pork barrel spending: Clinton and Obama are weak-kneed: McCain is strong.

Posted 3/11/08

THE SEER

Former House Majority Leader and presidential candidate, Dick Gephardt, warned back in February 1, 2001: that the Bush's tax plan: "**threatens our prosperity and could return us to the big deficits of the 1980s. I, for one, have learned a valuable lesson from the 1991 Reagan tax cuts. I do not intend to repeat that mistake.**"

Fast forward to March 10, 2008: 1.35 million homes went into foreclosure in 2007, economic growth showed a sharp downturn in the fourth quarter of 2007, the Dow has lost more than 2,000 points, the dollar has hit a record low vs. the euro, inflation is up 4.1 percent, and 63,000 jobs were lost last month, the most in five years. Some economists think we are in a recession. And, as of March 1, 2008, the National Deficit: has climbed to $9,346,333,640,000. The three Bush tax cuts favoring the wealthy—to help workers and stimulate the economy are a failure. It created a monstrous federal debt. The interest on the national debt for the first five months of fiscal year 2008: $198,517,767,159.

The three Bush tax cuts: basically, were a greedy plan to cut taxes on the wealthy—because, they had the power in congress to do so—and used false arguments to justified it. It is the Republican agenda. Mc Cain—wants to make the Bush tax cuts permanent. He rather have Bush's endorsement—than, listen to his conscience. Without a tax raise, the National Debt will continue to climb for the next four years—to New Record Heights.

Posted 3/12/08

AMERICANS ARE SUCKERS FOR TAX-CUTTERS

They voted for Reagan over Mondale.

They voted for Bush over Al Gore.

They voted for Bush over Kerry.

Now, they are looking at a $9.3 trillion US National Debt. Cutting essential public services to reduce the deficit, the Schwarzenegger and Bush strategy is not acceptable, while some Americans are multimillionaires and billionaires.

Professor Robert Reich states in his blog: "Income and wealth have become more concentrated than any at any time in the past 80 years." That is not good. One major reason: the Reagan and Bush tax cuts. In 2007, the wealth of the lowest ranked 400 richest Americans: $1.3 billion. That is up $300 million from the previous year. Their combined wealth: $1.54 trillion--and Bush cut their income, dividend, capital gains, and estate tax. That is wrong, when the rich are getting fabulously richer, 47 million Americans have no medical coverage—and the National Debt—is exploding. Rather than raise tax cuts on the wealthy—Bush raised the debt ceiling to $9.85 trillion. That is the wrong solution.

He is pushing his problem—on the next president.

Robert Reich, the former Secretary of Labor and now professor at Berkeley, advised back in February of 2001: **"No Tax Cuts. Period."** Even Senator John McCain voted NO on the Bush tax cuts and said: a disproportional amount went to the wealthy. But once, the deficit surfaced and the Iraq war commenced—a tax increase, disproportional, going to the wealthy—should have been enacted. But, McCain—did just the opposite: he voted YES on extending the dividend and capital gains tax cut. This was an immoral tax cut; because, soldiers were being killed and maimed in Afghanistan and Iraq war—while the super rich—back home--gave themselves a tax cut: made no sacrifice (in support of the war). McCain—forsook his conscience--to prove he was a loyal Republican—and voted for the most immoral tax cut of all times. It is reprehensible.

THE FEDERAL BUDGET DECEPTION

Since, Ronald Reagan took office, the US government has been spending the Social Security paid-in-surplus--off-budget on things not intended--and reporting to the American people—a bogus federal deficit. In a few years, these benefits will come due—and US government must tax the people to pay for them. Because, there is nothing in the Social Security Trust Fund—except IOUs. These bogus budget deficits were used by Bush--to convince the people: his tax cuts were working. During the last seven years--the top 1 percent gained enormous tax savings--while the US National Debt—skyrocketed.

The Enron Corporation used the same method of accounting: keeping shareholders and investors blindfolded about off-the-books partnerships--called: "Raptors (birds of prey)," that materially affected the annual reports (i.e., liabilities were larger and the profits were smaller than reported). It, eventually, imploded and employees and shareholders lost billions—while, some executives profited.

US Federal government is doing the same thing: it is keeping a false set of books. Here are the figures:

- 2001: the government reported a $128 billion budget surplus, when, in fact, you add Social Security paid-in surplus of $150 billion spent off-budget: there was a $21.7 billion deficit.

- 2002: the government reported a $157 billion budget deficit. The Bush administration failed to mention: it spent the SS paid-in-surplus of $158 billion—off budget. The total federal deficit: $421 billion.

- 2003: the government reported a $374 billion budget deficit. The Bush administration failed to mention: it spent the $168 billion paid in SS Surplus off-budget: The total federal deficit: $555 billion

- 2004: the government reported a $412 billion budget deficit. The Bush administration failed to mention it spent the SS paid-in-surplus of $178 billion off budget. The total deficit: $596--and so forth.

Here is what Bush said (Oct. 11, 2006): "This morning my administration released the budget number for fiscal 2006." -- "These numbers show that the budget deficit has been reduced to $248." He failed to mention: the $200 billion paid-in-SS surplus was spent off budget. The total deficit: $574.

Bush did this seven years in row: reported a bogus government deficit to the American people. It is an incomplete deficit—it does not include the off-budget expenses—paid for by the Social Security paid in surplus. It took paid in cash—and replaced it with IOUs. That is fraud.

What is needed—an investigation and the prosecution of Bush—if, indeed, he misled the people—the same—as Ken Lay. The US government should come clean--and state what these off-budget expenses are--and report the total yearly deficit of the US government. The US president should be 100 percent honest—not just – one-half. And what is worst: Bush vowed to put the Social Security paid-in-surplus in a "lockbox" in his presidential campaign in 2000. Every year, he spent it—and reported a bogus deficit to the American people.

At no time: did he tell the people—the whole truth.

Posted 3/14/08

THE MASS MEDIA IS GUILTY!

The mass media—has failed to report the US budget deception to the taxpayers. They have been hoodwinked. The reason: corporate executives, talk show hosts, and news casters are the big beneficiaries of the Bush tax cuts. They are highly paid: not to rock the boat—or endanger their big tax-breaks. And this was made evident by the last presidential debate between Clinton and Obama (in Ohio): conducted by NBC's Brian Williams and Tim Russert—they did not ask one question about tax issues, the deficit, etc.

And this is an important issue; because, the $88 billion budget deficit for the first four months of fiscal 2008—is double that of 2007. This has a huge impact on the economy and the dollar.

So far, in all the presidential debates that I have seen or read: not once—has a candidate been asked: whether they would continue to:

- raid the paid-in Social Security surplus to pay for off-budget expense

- use a fraudulent method of accounting by keeping government expenses off-budget

- and reporting a phony partial deficit to the American people (i.e., making it smaller, than it is)—like Bush has done for seven years.

I believe: the US government—should halt this practice of deceiving American taxpayer and give a full accounting.

I have sent my book to more than 40 top journalists—including Brian Williams--and not one has made my allegations or facts—known to the public. What makes the news: Britney Spears—not my book.

Posted 3/17/08

THE BUDGET--DEBT GAP!

Senate Budget Committee Chairman, Kent Conrad, D – N.D., said: that Bush would "go down in history as the most fiscally irresponsible president ever. That fact is, that the nation's debt has exploded in his watch – rising $3 trillion since 2001, to $9 trillion today."

But, the problem is more serious than that: there is gross deception—in reporting federal budget deficits. There is fraud—in the way: the government--keeps books. It keeps books like the Enron Corporation.

Its annual budget deficits are partial. It disguises the true cost of government: by spending the S.S. surplus off-budget.

Bush used the 2001—reported phony budget surplus--as pretext to rebate money and cut taxes on the wealthy.

In fact, there was no surplus. And he continued to do this for the next six years—spending the SS paid-in-surplus—off budget—and reporting an incomplete federal deficit—to voters.

The off-budget expenses are kept secret. I can not find them on the Internet, in the Time Almanac, or the STATISTICAL ABSTRACT OF THE UNITED STATES. They exist, because—there is a big gap between the official budget deficit of $168 billion for FY 2007—and the debt increase over the prior year: $501 billion. The way Bush makes the budget deficit—smaller—he leaves government expenses off the budget. That is deceiving the taxpayer (or voters). The CBO should explain the $333 billion gap.

January 16, 2008: The Comptroller General of the US, David Walker, warned of

America's looming bankruptcy. He states: social security, Medicare, and federal pension debt—is approaching--$72 trillion.

The off-budget spending of the Social Security paid-in-surplus for the last 22 years, as of March 2008--created a $2.3 trillion debt. Real money has been siphoned out of the SS Trusts Funds and replaced with non-negotiable bonds. This money has been spent off-budget by the US government for things—not originally intended by the FICA payroll deductions and reported false federal deficits to the voters. But, the hidden debt is many times larger.

McCain is either blind, stupid or insane—to pledge no new taxes. Unless taxes are raised—combined with cuts in excessive entitlements and waste--the federal deficit will continue to climb until it—implodes. Bush's pro-growth policies: have led to huge growth in the deficit. It is like putting more weight on a horse—until it collapses.

We—now—must pay for 22 years of deceit! As the end of fiscal year: 2007: the SS IOUs—will add $26,328 in debt to a family of four.

Posted 3/18/087

THE DEATH TAX

(revised)

The Death Tax is a derogatory term for the estate tax. (Some) plutocrats and misinformed people want it repealed. It is a tax on the estate of the decedent—before assets are transferred to heirs or recipients. It was a pre-paid progressive inheritance tax. It was a fair tax (until it was butchered by congress).

Reason # 1: When, there is a National Debt—or government budget deficit--that means: there was under taxation. Therefore, when the rich man dies, it is fair to collect back taxes--owed.

Reason # 2: the country's natural resources, government services, and labor of others: contribute to wealth building; therefore, they deserve a share.

Reason # 3: untaxed (large) transfers of wealth—creates a class of people that pay little or no tax—and enjoy the resources of the nation and services of the governments: defense, the congress, courts, interstate highways, education, etc. It is unethical to tax labor—and not inherited income.

18

Reason # 4: the repeal of the estate tax creates two classes of people: those that pay taxes on labor--and those that receive tax-free inherited wealth.

Reason # 5: the repeal of the estate (or inheritance) tax--makes it possible to transfer huge amounts of wealth (or income) from generation to generation--creating a perpetual American aristocracy that becomes richer and richer (i.e., from investments) and pays little or no taxes.

Reason # 6: the concentration of wealth in the hands of a few is bad: it creates a nation ruled by the Super-Rich.

McCain---is the only candidate left in the presidential race: that voted YES—on the repeal of the death tax. He is a little of the dumb side. He serves a group of plutocrats--not the majority of people. He said in the senate debate of HR-8: he did not support the repeal from the outset, but he changed his mind. That was a major goal of the Bush Administration. And he gave false arguments—to do so:

To protect family farms and businesses: A CBO report shows: that if, the exemption is set at $2 million, only 123 farms and 135 family-owned businesses would be subject to the tax. The exemption, in 2006: $2 million for singles: $4 million for married couples. Neil Harl, an Iowa State University economist, says: "It is a myth" that family farms are lost to the estate tax.

He argued: tax receipts were up 11.2 percent for the first seven months of 2006—and that was proof, the Bush tax cuts were working—and reason enough: to get rid of the estate tax. He failed to mention: five years of federal budget deficits—or the soaring National debt--at the time around: $8.4 trillion—were proof: the Bush tax cuts were not working.

He says: it's a matter of fairness—to get rid of the death tax—referring to the estate tax. That is opposite what President Theodore Roosevelt said in his State of the Union address in 1906: "The man of great wealth owes a peculiar obligation to the state, because he derives special advantage from the mere existence of the government." He argued in favor of the estate (or inheritance) tax.

McCain said: "It is simply unfair for death to be a taxable event". Why not, if one dies—and leaves a large estate. But, the fact is: the exemption for 2006-8: excludes 99.5 percent of Americans. The death tax is a term, he used to malign the estate tax—a tax on the large taxable assets of the decedent—before it is transferred to heirs. It seldom, affects family businesses and farms. However, its repeal—would save Lee Raymond, the former CEO of Exxon Mobile, $164 million, or Vice President Cheney, up to $60 million, etc.

He quoted a poll: that suggests 68 percent of Americans support repealing the death tax. That poll is not valid, because, there was a public relations campaign funded by wealthy families—to turn people against it. McCain used some of these false arguments. Once, enlightened: the majority will favor keeping it. These people spent $200 million lobbying on Capital Hill to repeal the estate tax. McCain seems to be working for them. Everything, he said: was either distorted—or false.

McCain voted YES—on raising the estate tax exemption to $5 million: Clinton and Obama: NO. McCain has the wrong vision for America: he does not believe in the principle of fairness, the collection of back taxes owed, or the common good—(i.e., dividing the pie with the others).

Hillary Clinton—also has some royal blood in veins: she favors making the 2009 Bush estate tax exemption of $3.5 million for individuals and $7 million for married couples--permanent. That is a little less bad for the nation; only, 1/3 of 1 percent would be subject to the estate tax. You mean to say: estates with a net worth of $3.5 million for individuals and $7 million for couples--owes no back taxes, when we have a $9.3 trillion federal deficit created in their life-time: including her and Bill. Bill Clinton—has admitted to being under taxed. Do you believe: recipients—of up to $7 million--should pay no tax? Hillary does. I don't know where Obama stands—on this issue

I know this: both Clinton and Obama voted NO--on the repeal of the estate tax; but, Obama made a statement.

He said: "This is shameful. Are we really going to cut taxes again for the Forbes 400 before we fix the alternative minimum tax which affects middle-class families? Are we really going to cut taxes for multimillionaires and billionaires before we extend the expiring child tax credit which helps working families? Are we really going to worsen our country's financial future for all Americans just so that a tiny number of the estates—estates that average over $13 million—can escape all taxes."

Hillary Clinton made no statement.

The problem with the present estate tax: it is not progressive; because the lower tax rates have been eliminated by increases in the exemptions build-in the Bush 2001 $1.35 trillion tax cuts. The CTJ states: over 52 percent of these tax cuts will go to the top 1 percent--an average $342,000 each over the decade. These do not include: the Bush: $330 billion 2003 and $70 billion 2005 extension of the dividend and capital gains tax cuts (heavily favoring the rich). This under taxation began with Reagan. On top of this: there is excessive compensation at the top. Carl Icahn, recently, criticized the fat paychecks of CEOs who did a terrible job and called them "morons." I see them as 21[ft] century Robber Barons.

Here are three prime examples: the CEO of Citigroup, Merrill Lynch, and Countrywide Financial: they all reaped huge rewards—while their companies suffered billion dollar losses.

The real losers: shareholders and taxpayers.

The fact, that CEOs succeed in keeping excessive and unmerited compensation --is proof—the government is ruled by a corrupt plutocracy: the statutes (or courts) permit it. The CEO heist is well documented. Yet, there have been no changes in the law—or prosecutions of these figures.

The only heirs—that should get an exemption up to $2 million: double for couples: from the estate tax are those that inherit and operate family farms or businesses. I believe the top 1 to 5 percent should be subject to a progressive estate (or inheritance) tax. Revenues from this source—will help reduce the deficit—and fund needed government programs.

See my book: **"The Estate Tax and Politics"** for more details.

Posted 3/19/08

THE ADDENDUM

The argument: that the estate (or death) tax is double taxation is wrong. Reason:

#1. The income tax is a tax on the individual—and pays the cost of government —for one generation—not two, or three, etc.

#2. The inheritance tax—pays the cost of government: for those who receive inherited income (or wealth)—or the next generation.

The repeal of the estate or inheritance tax—permits the next generation to avoid paying the cost of government—while enjoying its benefits and services. That is wrong.

Tax-free family trusts—does this (also).

Posted 4/1/08

TWO CRISES

The skyrocketing housing foreclosure crisis and the soaring National Debt are similar in many ways.

In 2000: Edward M. Gramlick, Federal Reserve Board member warned of the dangers of sub-prime lending practices.

This was ignored. Bush also ignored warnings his tax cuts—would create federal deficits.

The housing foreclosure crisis is based on an assumption that house prices would continue to rise: they did not.

Likewise--Bush thinks: cutting taxes—will increase economic growth—but, what happened: the National Debt grew faster. And he maintains: he is right. His head is buried in the sand. The National debt—is zooming towards $10 trillion and higher. Still, he wants to make the tax cuts on the rich and super-rich—permanent.

He is a diehard plutocrat.

The only people—that can easily afford—a tax increase are the rich and the super-rich. In the midst of rising home foreclosures: I read in the LA times: leases of beach front homes in Malibu—costing up to $150,000 a month—are going fast.

It also stated: the housing market troubles haven't touched homes valued at $10 million or more.

Wealth is concentrated at the top.

The growing huge US Debt is responsible in part: for the sputtering economy—that could nosedive. It is similar to the housing foreclosure crisis: debt is growing faster than revenues.

And, the stimulus package costing $150 billion—to spur the economy—is digging a deeper hole. It is unfunded. It is a job half-done. It did not raise taxes on the wealthy—to pay for it. They have been woefully under taxed—for the last 28 years.

It is like taking out a piggy-back loan—to pay bills—or buy a house. It is based on an assumption: things will get better.

But, the truth of the matter, sometimes things get worst: pollution, globe warming, hurricanes, rapid depletion of natural resources, rising prices, unemployment, etc.

The growing US National Debt—like the housing mortgage meltdown: will become devastating--if ignored.

2008—is going to be a bad year—for the deficit.

The housing bubble-burst was cased by deregulation, predatory lending, over indebtedness, etc. –and Blush allowed it to gain momentum. He gambled: letting mortgage lenders regulate themselves would help to expand the economy and justify his tax cuts. It blew-up in his face.

Cutting taxes—mostly on the wealthy—to stimulate the economy is also a flawed strategy --based on class greed and deception.

I say, it is better--if the fabulously rich are less rich—and the US Deficit is lower. That means: reversing the Bush tax cuts.

THE PROBLEM

Quote from Sam Pizzigati's Verist Paper No. 1—titled: "Reining in the CEOs, Plutocrats & Robber Barons -- The Second time around." He said:

"Overall, in 1943, the richest 2,500 Americans, after exploiting every loophole they could find, paid 78 percent of their total incomes in federal income tax."

"How does that compare today? Last year, our richest Americans, after exploiting every loophole they could find, paid 17.5 percent of their incomes in federal income tax."

The two main culprits: the Reagan and Bush tax cuts on the wealthy:

Reagan (1981 to 1989):

Class I:

1. The elimination of the 70% income tax bracket

2. The elimination of the 68% income tax bracket

3. The elimination of the 64% income tax bracket

4. The elimination of the 59% income tax bracket

5. The elimination of the 54% income tax bracket

6. The elimination of the 49% income tax bracket

7. The elimination of the 43% income tax bracket

8. The elimination of the 37% income tax bracket

9. The elimination of the 32% income tax bracket

10. **The enactment of the 28% income tax top rate.**

Class II

1. Increased the yearly gift tax exclusion: from $3,000 to $10,000

2. Increased the estate tax exemption: from $175,000—to $625,000.

Bush (2001 to 2009)

1. Reduced the top income tax rate from 39.6% to 35%

2. Reduced the capital gains tax from 20 to 15 percent*

3. Changed the taxation of dividends—from income to15 percent. *

4. Increased the annual gift tax exclusion from $10,000 to $12,000.

5. Increased the estate tax exemption in steps: from $675,000 to $3,500,000

6. Reduced the top estate tax rate from 55% to 45%.

7. Repealed the estate tax for the year 2010.

8. Phased out the limitation on itemized and personal deductions for incomes—over $100,000—by 2010

9. Tried, repeatedly, to permanently repeal the estate tax—called by Bush—the "Death Tax".

Two major consequences of these tax cuts: the rich have become super fabulously rich: the US National Debt—has climbed from $995 billion in 1980 to a staggering $9.4 trillion in 2008, and is growing at the rate of $1.7 billion a day.

*Note: over half—54 percent—of dividend and capital gains income flows to 0.2 percent of households with incomes over $1 million. Only 4 percent of this income flows to the 64 percent of households that have income of less than $50,000. This is a tax cut on the super rich.

RALPH NADER

I agree with five things (i.e., related to taxes) said by Ralph Nader—when he announced his bid for the presidency—on Meet the Press: Feb. 24, 2008.

#1: The complicity of the Democrats in not—"stopping him (Bush) on the tax cuts."

#2: "Why aren't we taxing speculation on Wall Street instead of heavily taxing human labor." What this refers to--is wages and salaries are subject to the top income tax of 35 percent; but, capital gains—15 percent. And the fact: that corporate executives and hedge-fund managers—take compensation in capital gains.

#3: "...and (why are we) putting huge deficits on the backs of our children and our grand children."

#4: And he said: "There is no debate on this"---And that was evident: NBC's Tim Russert: asked no questions—avoided the subject.

#5: He said: fifteen hundred corporations get their way from the majority of 535 members of congress (i.e., over the interest of the people). This can by seen: by the fact: corporations are paying less and less corporate income tax, while their profits have been increasing.

TICKLE-DOWN ECONOMICS

Bush's argument—cutting taxes, disproportionately, on the wealthy—will help workers, create jobs, and fuel the economic is spurious. It might help some, but what it did: it created a bigger national debt—and weakened the dollar. It also resulted in higher state taxes and cuts in social programs to reduce the deficit. The top income tax rate from 1944 to 1980—had a range of 94 % to 70%--and the ratio of national debt to GDP fell from 114 percent to 33 percent during the same period. Whereas, Reagan cut the top income tax rate from 70% to 28% and Bush from 39.6% to 35% and the ratio of national debt to GDP rose from 33 percent to 70 percent. Conclusion: the Bush's tax cuts favoring the richest Americans to help workers are a SCAM. The rich are richer: the workers are worst off. Home foreclosures are up, the cost of living is up, the unemployment rate is up, the National Debt is up, etc.

Posted 4/8/08

TWO INDISPENSABLE TAX PRINCIPLES

President Theodore Roosevelt said in a June 1907 speech: "Most great civilized countries have an income tax and an inheritance tax. In my judgment both should be part of our system."

But, what Reagan and Bush have done--is nearly abolish both: the nine top income tax rates and brackets were eliminated by Reagan and Bush lowered the top four remaining marginal tax rates.

And, both significantly raised the estate tax exemption: Reagan from $175,000 in 1981 to $625,000 in 1988. Bush further increased the exemption from $675,000 in 2001 to $1,000,000 in 2002-3, to $1,500,000 in 2004-5, to $2,000,000 in 2006-8, and $3,500,000 in 2009. This, greatly, increases the amount of wealth (or income) that can be transferred to the next generation tax-free. Bush also lowered the top estate tax rate from 55% to 45%. He, also, succeeded in repealing the estate tax for the year: 2010.

The graduating income tax—is now—basically a semi-flat tax and the estate tax—has been nearly phased out. Its permanent repeal—is a top priority of the Bush Administration. He is a thoroughbred plutocrat. He believes in an America—ruled by dynastic wealth and political power.

Allan Sloan, Wall Street editor of Newsweek, put it this way: "President Bush [i.e., by repealing the estate tax] would create a new class of landed aristocrats who would inherit billions tax-free, invest the money, watch it compound tax-free, and hand it down tax-free to their heirs."

President Franklin Roosevelt said in a speech to Congress on June 19, 1935: "In the last analysis such accumulations [of inherited wealth] amount to the perpetuation of great and undesirable concentration of control in a relatively few individuals---Such inherited economic power is as inconsistent with the ideals of this generation as inherited political power was inconsistent with the ideals of the generation which established our Government."

King George Bush—you are fired!

TWO CHOICES

Ralph Nader says: "Democracy or avaricious plutocracy, that is the question." Here is what a plutocracy does: right off the bat--cut their taxes, tries to repeal the estate tax, cuts social programs, resists efforts to raise the minimum wage, raise their wages, overlook corporate fraud, ignores the will of the people, tramples on human rights, tries to rig elections, put profits first—before environmental safeguards, thwarts efforts to gain information— about—their possible secret illegal activities, appoints an Attorney General—who is a friend, practices political favoritism, gives pardons to political friends or allies, punishes whistleblowers, takes the Fifth—when questioned about internal activities, caters to large corporations over the interest of the people, fails to do anything about excessive executive compensation, maintains a health care (or medical) system that profits from human sickness, designs and prescribes drugs that mimics illegal, buys out and controls the mass media, blocks debates about fair tax reform, squanders taxpayer dollars, lets the deficit grow—rather than—pay their fair share of taxes—for wars—they start, distort facts in State of Union Addresses, etc. **Does that sound familiar?**

Posted 4/10/18

THE GIFT TAX

(revised)

"Briefly stated, the annual exclusion is the single largest loophole in the transfer tax system, and it has, in effect, converted the U.S. comprehensive estate and gift tax scheme into a system of welfare for the wealthy. If Congress is serious about reforming U.S. welfare programs, the annual exclusion should be a key part of Such reform." ---Professor Jeffrey Kinsler

The gift tax is written backwards. It taxes the giver of gifts—rather than the recipient. It was enacted to prevent the transfer of wealth during life—to avoid the estate tax at death. But, over the years: the annual exclusion was raised: from $3,000 in 1984 to $12,000 per year per donee--and $24,000 by gift splitting between married couples: double the minimum wage.

A couple can put in a trust fund—for a child or donee: $24,000 per year for 18 years: that would total: $432,000 tax-free.

These gifts are not charitable contributions--or the same as birthday, wedding, or holiday gifts. They are basically transfers of wealth—that allows the donee or recipient—to receive tax-free income. That is wrong; because, the recipient enjoys the benefits of government without paying for the cost. Therefore—these gifts—should be subject to a gift or transfer of wealth tax. Why should labor be taxed and income from non-labor—not taxed. The fact—that recipients do not work for these transfers of wealth: that is benefit enough.

If, income from wages, tips, interest, lottery and gambling winnings, dividends, unemployment compensation, bonuses, and alimony are taxed: why not—inter *vivos* transfers of wealth (or income) to the next generation. Why, should—they live on transferred tax-free income or wealth created by a previous generation. Taxes paid by parents or progenitors--do not pay the cost of government for their children and grandchildren—or future generations.

The way the current US gift tax is designed and manipulated—it makes it possible, for the wealthy to make large transfers of wealth to the next generation and avoid the gift, estate, and income tax.

In 2008, the donor can make an annual gift of $12,000 to any number of persons ($24,000 for couples) without incurring any gift tax. That decreases the size of the estate—subject to the estate tax. And the donee or recipient can receive any amount of gift or inheritance without paying any income tax. That is wrong: two generations living on the taxes paid by one.

And, there are more tax-free gifts:

The cost of tuition and medical expenses. When, you add to that: the annual tax-free gift: $13,000/$26,000 in 2009: that is too much.

On top of this: you can exceed the annual per donee limit up to $1 million during your life-time without incurring any gift tax ($2 million for married couples). All of this is tax-free to the recipient—or recipients.

This is part of the 2001-Bush tax cuts.

I believe the inter *vivos* transfers of wealth or income should be taxed as income—or a bank or trust account set up--between donor and recipient; so, these gifts or transfers of wealth—can be made: subject to a gift tax at the time of the transfer—where the donee—or the donor and donee are held jointly liable for the payment--excluding customary small to medium size gifts. A gift tax—is preferable; because—of income tax deductions. **That is fair for these and other reasons.**

The present gift tax rates are fair; except, they don't apply to the estate tax; because—gifts are annual and inheritances are life-time. I might add: that the Netherlands taxes the donee for gifts and inheritances. That is more correct than taxing the giver of gifts. The US unified gift and estate tax and its exemption increases is--really--a well designed tax evasion scheme by plutocrats—so that the donor and the donee—pay little or no gift or estate (or inheritance) tax.

It is not fair; when, one class lives on transferred tax-free income (or bequests)—and one pays taxes on income from labor.

Posted 4/22/08

PLUTOCRATS DISLIKE THE CAPITAL GAINS TAX

ABC's Charles Gibson, as chief moderator of the democratic presidential debate at Philadelphia, represented the interests of the ruling plutocracy—not the majority of people.

When, he asked Obama: "You have however said you would favor an increase in the capital gains tax." The reason why, this is such an important question to the ruling plutocracy—a big percentage of their wealth and income comes from capital gains—or investments. Ninety percent of capital wealth—is own by the top 10 percent—according to a Fed's survey.

But, he made it look like a general concern of the people--by saying: "So why raise it all, especially given the fact that 100 million people in this country own stock and would be affected." But, this is—misleading: the wealthiest 10 received 90 of the capital gains eligible for this special tax cut. That is why—this is such an important issue to the rich. And, Charles Gibson, being in this group, set about to attack Obama's capital gains tax-increase proposal, when he said: "So why raise it at all…" And, this was predicated on his argument, saying: "And in each instance, when the rate dropped, revenues from the tax increased."

He is, probably, referring to two instances:

The first in 1997, when the capital gains tax was reduced from 28% to 20%. But, this argument is flawed. Tax revenues went up—because, there was a stock market boom taking place in the nineties. Capital gains revenues—also went up from 1993 to 1998, significantly—when the capital gains tax was 28 percent. And his argument; also, is flawed; because, capital gains tax revenues plummeted from 2001 to 2003—when the stock market headed down.

Secondly, Mr. Gibson argued: capital gains revenues went up, when Bush lowered the capital gains tax from 20 to 15 percent in 2003. But, again: there was a stock market boom between 2003 and 2007: that made capital gains possible.

Reason 2: investors increase their investments in the stock market during upswings—increasing profits.

29

Reason 3: there was a boom in real estate prices--during this period: that also gave a boost to capital gains revenues.

Reason 4: the government lowered the federal funds rate to 1% in 2003: that helped spur the economy

Reason 5: defense spending went up during the Iraq War—that commenced in 2003—that fueled the economy.

Reason 6: the government borrowed money to pay its expenses—rather than tax the people and corporations: that had a temporary—stimulating effect: that now has a negative effect: the massive National Debt.

Reason 7: the reduction in the capital gains tax was at the bottom of a stock market cycle—and captured its upward movement: making it possible for capital gains—to take place.

Proof: lowering the capital gains tax—does not, necessarily, increase capital gains revenues: 2008 is going to be a down year for capital gains revenues; because, of the fall of stock and real estate prices.

Conclusion: capital gains revenues increase and decrease with the rise and fall of the stock market; more so, than, lowering the capital gains tax. Also, there is the question of fairness--when lowering capital gains tax—lowered than the tax of labor, private businesses, and corporations. And I think Obama brought that out; when, he mentioned: that the top 50 hedge fund mangers made $29 billion last year—and pay a lower tax than their secretaries. And he said: "That's not fair." That must be corrected.

Posted 5/5/08

CAPITAL GAINS TAX

(revised)

Originally, capital gains were taxed as income from 1916 to 1921 and reached a high of 77 percent. From 1922 to 1934: it was 12.5 percent for assets held 2 years. Since then, capital gains tax has undergone numerous modifications in terms of rates, exclusions, and holding periods. In 1976-77—the maximum long-term capital gains tax rate was 39.875%. Later, it was reduced to 28 percent—and to 20 percent. In 2003, Bush reduced it to 15 percent.

OECD countries that have a higher individual long-term capital gains tax rates 2005-2006—than the United States.*

Denmark: 43%

United Kingdom 32%

Sweden 30%

Finland 28%

Norway 28%

Japan 26%

Hungary 25%

Germany 0%--beginning in 2009: 25%

Australia 23.5%

Ireland 20%

Poland 19%

France 17.6%

* **Source: accf.org**

Mexico 0%: great inequality in the distribution of income: the lowest 10% share: 1.4%, the highest 10% share: 42.8 % (Survey 1995). Carlos Slims Helu—the new richest man in the world: worth $59 billion. In the community of Netzahual-coyotl, on the outskirts of Mexico City, over 1,000,000 lower-class Mexicans live in single-room brick structures erected on land that floods when it rains. They have few public services, no unemployment compensation, and the poor do not receive welfare payments.

For the US: I have proposed a graduating: 15, 25, and 35 percent capital gains tax--based on current conditions: the National Debt, the war in Iraq, and the fact: in 2005, the wealthiest 1 percent with income of over $396,000 received almost 70 percent of the long-term capital gains.

The position of the three presidential candidates on the taxation of capital gains—still in the race.

Senator McCain: make permanent the Bush tax cuts: 15 percent capital gains tax. He stated on *This Week:* cutting taxes is more important than a balanced budget. That is Bush's sentiments: he will add close to $4 trillion to the National Debt by the end of 2008.

Senator Obama said: "I certainly would not go above what existed under Bill Clinton, which was 28 percent"

Senator Clinton: "I wouldn't raise it above 20 percent if I raised it at all." She is somewhat ambiguous—or not forthright.

OUT OF THE RACE:

Democratic presidential candidate John Edwards proposed raising the capital gains tax to 28 percent.

THE GOLD STANDARD

(revised)

The tax code must be based on economic principles, fair, produce enough revenues to pay for government outlays—and the government must render certain basic services to the people: such as: health, education, welfare, and security. That is not all true of the US Tax Code.

The most glaring example—is the taxation of Hedge Fund managers. The top 20, in 2006, pocketed an average income of $657.5 million or 22,255 times the pay of the average U.S. worker. And their compensation—in the form of carried interest (i.e., a share of the funds earnings)--is taxed at the capital gains rate of 15%. That is blatantly—wrong.

Representative Levin (D-MI) introduced: HR 2834: that would tax Carried Interest as ordinary income. That is more fair. Also, Carried Interest is not a capital gain—of the fund's manager. It is capital gains on the investments of outside partners.

It fits compensation—more. Remember: the manager of these funds are also investors. So, I don't think: they should get long-term capital gains taxation on the investments of others—when it, applies to their compensation, and their investment too—or at least—a good argument.

I might add: Clinton, Obama, and former presidential candidate John Edwards: back taxing Carried Interest as regular income—as a matter of fairness: citing the disparity of the compensation of Equity Fund managers and labor--or Warren Buffett and his secretary.

That makes the change—imperative.

Raising the capital gains tax to 35% over $500,000 would serve the same purpose.

But, HR 2834 does not solve the problem completely, because the US income tax is only progressive to the middle. It must be progressive to at the top. Incomes of the top 1 percent have skyrocketed, but the marginal income tax rates have not been raised—correspondingly.

Taxing income--in the hundreds of millions of dollars at the rate of 35 percent—is not enough. The Tax Code needs a complete overhaul.

I believe the graduating income marginal tax rates to 70 percent—matches the Gold Standard. If, that is true: the present top income tax rate of 35 percent is too low, as well as, the 15 percent tax on long-term capital gains. These are the biggest inequities of the Tax Code.

There are two equal means of wealth building: capital and labor. Based on that premise:

What is the justification: for taxing capital gains and labor--unequally?

How, can you say: capital is more important than labor in the production of goods and services--or GDP?

Belgium has reputation for being a tax haven for the idle rich. Capital gains are exempt from taxation. However, the taxation of income from labor is 50% percent over 30,210 EUR--based on the current conversion rate--about $48,336. That is out of balance. It places the cost of government on the shoulders of workers.

The US—taxes income from labor and short term capital gains--equally. That is correct. What is wrong: the sudden drop in the taxation of long term capital gains: from 35 percent to 15. That is a big tax break for rich investors.

What it does—it separates long-term capital gains from the income tax table—and fixes the tax at an arbitrary—low flat rate.

I believe a sliding or tapered exclusion should apply to long-term capital gains—and kept subject to the income tax tables.

What is the justification for taxing short term capital gains progressive—and long-term flat? The U.S. tax code does—for the most part.

There is more too this…

Posted 5/7/08

1 DAY—MAKES BIG TAX DIFFERENCE

(revised)

The 15 percent tax on capital gains—i.e., an asset bought and sold—1 day longer than 1 year--is a big tax break for the rich investor. In 2005, the wealthiest 1 percent of Americans received almost 70% all long-term capital gains. It does not work out that well for the bottom sixty percent: they received only 2%.

For those in the 25% income tax bracket: a 10% tax savings

For those in the 28% income tax bracket: a 13 % tax a saving

For those in the 33% income tax bracket: an 18 % tax savings

For those in the 35% income tax bracket: a 20% tax savings.

In word words: the higher your income—the bigger your tax-break. The difference between short and long term capital gains (i.e., 1 day)--neutralizes progressive taxation of capital gains for the top four brackets.

For example, a long-term capital gain of $1,000,000 would save the investor in the top income bracket: $200,000.

What is the justification?

One reason (given): the buy and sell did not take place within the span of a taxable year. That is weak, because, business profits, sometimes, take more than a year to achieve and there is no long-term profit tax and students spend 4 to 8 years in universities—before earning a living.

The second reason: long-term capital gains are diluted by inflation. But, the one day difference between short and long term: does not justify a drop in the tax on the top bracket: from 35% to 15%.

The third reason: it spurs the economy. That is weak and deceitful. What it spurs: investments in the stock market, real estate, etc.

I believe: a sliding exclusion of 10% per year up to 5 years for long-term capital gains or 5% per year for 12 years—allowing for inflation and subject to the marginal income tax rates is more fair. But, the US tax code is not fair and designed by plutocrats.

The biggest inequity: the 25 percent tax on income from wages: from $31,851 to $77,100--compared to the 15 percent tax of long-term capital gains from $31,851 to hundreds of millions—or billions.

The second biggest inequity: corporate executives, that receive stock options and stock awards—as compensation, instead of salary, to take advantage of the 15 percent tax on long-term capital gains.

These two big tax inequalities: stem from the 1 day difference in taxation of short and long term capita gains. The real reason: it enables the top 1 percent to make big investment profits--fast—and pay low taxes.

The Taxpayers Relief Act of 1997, retained the 28% capital gains tax up to 18 months, and it reduced the tax to 20% held 18 months to 5 years—and to 18% after five years. That is a fairer definition of long-term—it divided long-term into three time periods. But, that did not last long. It was changed to 12 months in 1998: plutocrats—want instant gratification.

The 20%, 40%, 60%, and 70% exclusion of capital gains held 1, 2, 5, and 10 years—of the Revenue Act of 1934—subject to the income tax rates--is far more reasonable (or fair)—than, compacting all long term capital gains into 366 days--and cutting the tax to 15 percent; mostly, benefiting the big-rich investor. In 2005, the middle 20 percent received only 1.1 % of the benefit.

The third rich man tax break: the exclusion of dividends and long-term capital gains from the Alternative Minimum Tax.

PRIVATE EQUITY AND HEDGE FUNDS

The taxation of long-term capital gains—at 15 percent, is particularly, immoral and pernicious, when it comes to Private Equity and Hedge Funds.

Private Equity Funds buy and sell equities in both the domestic and international markets. They also target distressed companies: buy, strip, and flip. Their tactics have been described as cold-blooded. Equity Funds create little or no goods and services. Basically, they are capitalistic parasites. Their main goal: high yield for investors. They are limited partnerships—not subject to the SEC. Many take advantage of offshore tax havens—to avoid US taxes. It requires a large sum of money to get in, and investors are kept confidently. They serve little or no useful purpose, except make a few men mega-rich--at the expenses of others. Some equity Fund managers have become billionaires. To prevent Equity Funds from growing in number and becoming Giant Financial Predators, that feed on the markets of the world or the labors of others— the capital gains tax needs reform.

It is not fair: that equity funds capital gains are taxed less, than, business or corporation profits—that produce goods and services—that, sometimes, takes years to research and develop.

It is not fair: that the compensation of Equity Fund mangers in the form of "carried interest"—sometimes in the hundreds of millions—are taxed at the long term capital gains rate of 15 percent—and ordinary income from labor—is taxed at 35 percent over $349,700 (2007).

It is not fair: that the difference between 1 day: should reduce the tax on capital gains: from 35% to 15%: benefiting the big-rich investor.

The 15% capital gains tax: rewards parasitism over capitalism.

Parasitism—siphons off profits from capitalism, the labors of others, and produce little and no goods and services.

The 15 percent capital gains tax: gives Equity Funds a competitive edge over corporations, whose top tax rate on profits is 35 percent and the profits of sole proprietorships-- that are taxed as income.

This—to a big degree—explains their explosion in number and size and the high compensation of fund mangers. Their goal: high yield and low taxation: from long-term capital gains: 1 day more than 1 year.

This tax—advantage: their cold-blooded tactics, lack of regulation, and greed: has led to these fantastic profits.

According to *Alpha* magazine: in 2006, the top 25 hedge fund mangers earned almost $14 billion.

It has become a world problem; for example: Luxembourg has no capital gains tax and is ranked #2 in the world for the number of Equity/Hedge funds registrations. Whereas, the income tax on labor: has 16 brackets: the highest: 39% over 34,500 EUR (2004). The cost of government falls on the shoulders of workers and investors are given a free ride.

Unions (worldwide) call private equity and hedge funds: "a cancer". Their main complaints: fund managers and partners are making fortunes by firing workers in LBOs and paying low taxes (on profits). Other complaints: paying big fees to takeover company executives, reducing worker benefits, stripping assets, neglecting environmental obligations, gutting important research and development projects, saddle these companies with high debt, and promptly existing with a large profit in an IPO. Investopedia says: "most of these IPOs do not perform very well."

Switzerland is the home of an estimated one-third of offshore funds. It has no tax on capital gains. And, it has the highest concentration of wealth in the top 10 percent--of any nation in the world.

In oil-rich Dubai—equity and hedge funds enjoy zero capital gains taxation—while Asian workers riot over mistreatment and low wages ($4 a day). It is a dynastic monarchy: good if, you're rich: not good, if, you are a worker. It built the tallest and most expensive hotel in the world for tourists—while, foreign workers live 8 in a room. It reminds me of egg-laying chickens crammed into cages without room to turn around—seen on TV.

McCain described Mitt Romney—after getting his endorsement—as the co-founder of Bain Capital, one of the nation's most successful private equity groups. But, one source on the Internet has a different opinion, it says: "Brain's tactics in business are not normal capitalism. They are similar to Hitler himself." Frankly—I don't have the facts—to pass judgment. I do believe: Equity Funds are under taxed and are like an invasion of locusts.

The same applies to Private Hedge Funds, which use a wide variety of short/long term investment strategies, such as: leverage, selling short, arbitrage, calculations by computer software programs, options, etc. Beside stocks and bonds: they take speculative positions in indexes, commodities and currencies. They also engage in LBOs and ruthless restructuring—and profiteering. They are unregulated (i.e., not required to file financial statements) and their trading practices are kept secret. They are called by Financial Journals: "barbarians at the gate."

What is needed: more regulation, more transparency, and higher taxation of capital gains--to prevent the cancer from spreading and undermining good capitalism that provide tangible human needs and services.

THE BIG RIP-OFF

Alpha Magazine reports: the top 25 hedge fund managers earned an average of $892 million in 2007—up from $532 million in 2006. The top five: over a billion and at the top of the list: John Paulson: $3.7 billion. One analyst puts it this way: 30 times in one hour—what the median family made all year. That was done—by betting short – on the ABX subprime mortgage index.

First of all: these capital gains (or profits) are not from the production of tangible goods or services. It is manufactured paper money (or profits) based, purely, on loss of value of something—or the fluctuation of abstract numbers. Taking a speculation position in indexes is not an investment in capitalism. It is parasitism: it feeds off of capitalism. It is capital gains without the production of goods and services. I am not even sure, selling short, is ethical (i.e., profiting from the loss of the value of something). President Herbert Hoover condemned it. I will leave that to one's conscience. The question here: should hedge/equity fund manager's performance fee be taxed at 15 percent—while the top rate for wages and salaries is 35 percent. Generally, Hedge Fund managers are compensated three ways:

The 2% fee: goes to expenses: rent, staff, office equipment, telephone bills, etc.

20% of profits: his compensation--as manager of the fund

His capital gains from personal investment in the fund.

Rep. Sander Levin's bill: HR 2834 (and 26 co-sponsors) would treat performance fees as ordinary income. That makes sense. It is a matter of fairness. This bill sits in limbo, because Bush has threatened to veto it.

Rep. Charles Rangel—included this provision in bill HR 3996. It was passed in the House: 216 to 193. All republicans voted against it.

The bill passed in the Senate—except, the provision taxing the performance fee of hedge/equity fund manager as ordinary income was deleted. This is proof: the US government is ruled by a cabal of rich men.

It is proof—capitalism has gone amuck!

BAD IDEA

(revised)

Of course, Senator McCain's proposed gas-tax holiday—is a bad idea. The 18.4 cents federal gas tax—per gallon—is not the problem. There are too many big engine, cars, pickups, vans, and SUVs on the road. Americans waste too much gas and oil company profits are excessive and under taxed. The gas-tax holiday is a foolish, vote-getting gimmick.

The LA Times states: the individual savings would be small and would result in a loss of as much as $9 billion in federal revenue for road and bridge construction.

Road builders say: the gas tax suspension could jeopardize more than 300,000 highway related jobs.

Lee Iacocca's gas-tax hike is a better idea: that would help build better roads, people would be more frugal, and that reduce traffic congestion. Countries that have a higher gas tax than the United States:

United Kingdom	$2.82	per gallon
France	$2.15	
Germany	$2.05	
Italy	$1.92	
Japan	$1.92	
Spain	$1.36	
Australia	$1.02	
Canada	$ .65	
New Zealand	$ .65	
United States	$ .38	

I think it is reprehensible of Bush's recent trip to the Middle East--to ask the Saudis to increase oil production and thereby, lower the price of gas—so, that we can continue our gas wasting habits. Some Americans think they have a right to waste the natural resources of the world.

For example, Governor Schwarzenegger flies regularly to work from Brentwood to Sacramento and back in a Gulfstream IV, that burns 512 gallons per hour and takes more than three hours. That is a big waste of jet-fuel and spews out as much as 4.9 metric tons of carbon dioxide per hour into the atmosphere—more than a car driven all year—or 8,000 miles. He has a free governor's penthouse in Sacramento, but he prefers to commute routinely—regardless of negative factors.

George Bush is the world's biggest fuel-waster. He has a fleet of jets and helicopters, that he uses for personal, political, and official transportation. He not only abuses this presidential perk, but, his gas polices are bad.

The people probably don't remember this—but, Bush cancelled the 2004 deadline for auto makers to develop prototype high-mileage cars—and the Bush Administration opposed efforts to close the $100,000 Hummer tax deduction, the biggest gas guzzler on road, and allowed the meager $1,500 tax deduction for fuel efficient hybrid vehicles to phase out.

The Hummer is the vehicle of choice of Schwarzenegger. The big engine GM, Ford, Chrysler vehicles are an American addiction. The only problem, we are wasting our natural oil resources—driving these vehicles.

Another reason for the high cost of gasoline—is Bush's economic, war, and tax polices, that has raised the National Debt and lowered the value of the USD compared to other world currencies: that raises the cost of imported oil. Since, Bush has been in office: the dollar has lost 80 percent of its value vs. the euro. And, since the price of OPEC oil is based on the USD: the price goes up as the dollar loses its value. Other reasons: increased demand and diminishing world oil reserves. McCain has dedicated himself—to carry out the same tax polices as Bush: that would be bad for the United States.

His gas-tax holiday is his first—bad idea.

Posted 5/22/08

TWO BAD US TRENDS

The first:

Since, 1967—the US Gini has increased from 39.7 to 47.0 in 2006. The Gini is a measurement of inequality of income distribution. And, those figures indicate: the share of income going to the top—is increasing—compared to the bottom during this period.

Nations with a good Gini:

Sweden 25.0...............2005

South Korea 31.6..........2006

Canada 32.1...............2005

France 32.5................2005

UK 36.0...................2005

Israel 38.6.................2005

Nations with a bad Gini:

Russia 41.3 2007

Philippines 45.8..............2006

China 47 2007

Mexico 50.9................2005

Brazil 56.7..................2005

South Africa 65... 2005

The second bad US trend:

The average income of the top 400 taxpayers: increased from $46.5 million in 1992 to $214 million in 2005. The perverse thing about this: the average tax paid: deceased from a high of 30% to 18% during the same period. If, you go back to the 1960s the trend is worst.

Tax reform is the main means of correcting these two bad US trends. According to SustainableMiddleClass.com: "the current maximum tax bracket is far too low and should be raised back to 70 percent."

WAS EX-CHAIRMAN OF THE FEDERAL RESERVE, ALAN GREENSPAN—A SAGE OR STOOGE?

In February 2000: Greenspan appeared before the Senate Banking Committee and recommended: the government use the federal surpluses to pay down the national debt (sage).

In 2001, working for the Bush administration, his advice to the U.S. Senate Committee: the 2001 Bush tax cuts were fiscally responsible, given the surpluses. Here, he is a stooge. Then, the Congressional Budget Office predicted the federal budget surplus would reduce the government debt by $5.6 trillion over the next 10 years. Greenspan said government estimates project more than enough surplus funds to pay off the debt and reduce taxes too.

Later, he defended backing Bush's 2001 tax cuts, saying: "We were all Wrong about the Surpluses". But, not every body was wrong: 153 members of the House voted against them—33 in the Senate.

This is part of what Senator Dodd said: "I hate to say this to my colleagues—I said it in 1981 (i.e., about the Reagan tax cuts); I will repeat it today, 20 years later—we are about to make the same mistake again."

Senator Kennedy: "They pretend that we can have it all—that this massive tax cut will not affect our ability to adequately fund our education and health care needs, to reduce the debt, and to financially strengthen Medicare and Social Security for future generations. This view is a fantasy. The reality is that this tax cut will have a direct and substantial effect on our ability to fulfill our responsibilities in each of these areas." And he said: "It is neither fair or affordable."

Senator Conrad: "We estimate that this bill, when combined with the real budget reflecting what will actually be spent over the next 10 years, will be raiding the Medicare trust fund by $311 billion and raiding the Social Security trust fund by $234 billion."

That is what happened!

Even Senator McCain said: "But I cannot in good conscience support a tax cut in which so many of the benefits go to the most fortunate among us, at the expense of middle class Americans who most need tax relief." But, he reversed himself--to run for the president on the republican ticket. He now, wants to make them permanent. If, they were not a good idea when there were surpluses: they, certainly, are a bad idea, after seven years of deficits. He sacrificed his good sense, to serve the republican agenda.

Senator Lieberman: "This tax cut squanders the hard-earned prosperity that our country has built over the last several years of historic economic growth. It returns us to the fiscal nightmare of the 1980s. This huge tax cut will bust the budget, resurrect the deep deficits of the past, and drive our economy into a ditch. For these reasons I will vote against this bill and urge my colleagues to do so as well."

Senator Rockefeller: "Finally, the sad fact is that this tax cut is now so large that it commits every dime of the surplus for tax cuts and current obligations, leaving nothing— 0—for Medicare solvency, new defense needs, or any other future or unanticipated emergencies."

Senator Wellstone: "Like the Reagan tax cuts of the early 1980s, this bill is too big, and fiscally irresponsible. It is grossly unfair. Its benefits go mostly to the wealthiest Americans. It will crowd out critical investments in education, health care, protecting the environment, energy conservation and renewables, and other key priorities for years to come."

Senator Durbin: "This bill on which we will be voting is based on the best guess of the economists for President Bush that we will have continued prosperity for the next 10 years—10 years. There is no economist who would wage their reputation on where we will be 10 months from now, let alone 10 years. It is based on pure speculation about anticipated surpluses, and that is a significant shortfall in the logic behind this tax cut."

Senator Byrd: "I fear that this tax cut will return us eventually to annual deficits and impede our efforts to retire the national debt."

That is what happened!

And he said: "History will hold us accountable for what we did here today in passing this monstrous tax cut. This tax cut, which mainly will benefit the wealthy, is based on pie-in-the-sky projected surpluses which probably will not materialize. History will not forget that the national needs of today and of future generations have been sacrificed for the sake of carrying out a political promise in the heat of political campaign last year."

So, not everybody was wrong.

In 2003: Alan Greenspan—rebutted many arguments in favor of Bush's second round of big new tax cuts. He testified before the Senate Banking Committee: "There is no question that as deficits go up, contrary to what some have said, it does affect long-term interest rates, it does have a negative impact on the economy, unless attended." That was contrary to what Vice President Cheney said to Treasury Secretary Paul O' Neil—after warning the Bush administration: growing budget deficits—pose a threat to the economy. He said: "You know, Paul, Reagan proved deficits don't matter." He was fired, shortly afterwards. One year after the 2001 Bush tax cuts: the surpluses failed to materialize.

For Greenspan's warning (or criticism): one Republican Senator—suggested Alan Greenspan should resign. However, his good advice was undone--by strongly supporting the elimination of the dividend tax—a key element of the 2003 Bush tax cuts. Here, he is dead wrong. The double taxation argument is not 100 percent valid. He is a forked tongued political hack—and a plutocrat in his heart. He was mute, hedged his statements, and agreed with some of the most the unfair and irresponsible tax cuts of all times.

He did not become heroic—until 2005; when, he warned: federal budget deficits were "unsustainable"—and urged Congress to solve the problem. They did not. That was too little–too late.

After resigning—in 2006: he expressed "remorse" that the Republicans followed his advice to lower taxes in 2001. He states: congress failed to change course—when the deficits appeared instead of surpluses—and harshly criticized Bush: for not vetoing bills that drove the country into deeper and deeper deficits. He says: "They swapped principle for power." So, did he.

Looking back—he is a Sage.

Posted 6/ 24/08

IS BARACK OBAMA—AN IDIOT?

(revised)

When I heard David Wessel on Washington Week state: Obama wants to apply the Social Security tax on wages above $250,000--I thought he made a mistake. I thought: Obama meant; when, he would raise taxes on those with incomes above $250,000—he was referring to the income tax. After a check--it is no mistake. That means: he is missing some synapses in his brain—or he is a potential Mugabe—when in office. He took farms from whites and gave them to blacks.

The Social Security tax on wages is 12.4%: half paid by the employee and half paid by the employer: that pays for retirement benefits for senior citizens.

In 2008, it is levied on wages up to $102,000. Its base has been raised yearly—an average of 4.1 percent since 1991—to reflect the increase in the consumer cost of living index. That is fair—because, benefits—have been increased.

Obama told senior citizens in Ohio: it is unfair for middle-class earners to pay the Social Security tax "on every dime they make," while millionaires and billionaires pay it only "a very small percentage of their income". He is wrong for a number of reasons—and it shows: he does not understand—how Social Security plan works.

1. It appears, he want the rich to pay for Social Security retirement benefits for the poor. But, that is not how it is structured. Your benefits are based on how much you pay in—unlike Medicare.

2. He wants to jump from the present ceiling—of $102,000—to tax wages over $250,000. But, those earning more than $250,000—do not need higher Social Security benefits.

3. Under his plan, every body would pay the Social Security tax on wages, except those earning from $102,000 to $250,000. That would be unfair and discriminatory.

4. And, those making more than $250,000 do not need higher Social Security retirement benefits. They can afford—private plans—and generally, the pay packages of executives—include pension plans.

5. The government should provide—a S.S. retirement plan for the lower and middle income worker—not for the wealthy.

6. Under his plan—the government would be paying higher benefits to those making over $250,000 a year—that don't need it.

7. It is not fair—to tax employers—to pay for (or subsidize) retirement benefit for non-employees. That is Obama's plan.

8. Presently, the paid-in Social Security tax exceeds benefits—paid out: there is a surplus. The problem—the U.S. government is spending that money on other government expenses. As of June 20, 2008: the Social Security paid-in-surplus totaled: $2,285,999,194,558.

9. There is no need to raise—the Social Security tax—at the present. The government needs to repay the Social Security Trust Fund—the amount it siphon-off, robbed- -or borrowed. It cannot do this by raising the Social Security tax on wages. It must come from other taxes lowered by Reagan and Bush. People like Bill Gates and Warren Buffett—who give away their money before they die, put it in a family trust—or make inter *vivo* gifts to their siblings are escaping their responsibility to repay the Social Security Trusts Funds—the money—U.S. government purloined—to make cuts in their income, dividend, capital gains, gift, and estate taxes. In other words: the S.S. paid-in-surplus—was transferred to them—by tax cuts. The Bush—repeal of the Death (or Estate) Tax for the year 2010--prevents the government from collected back taxes owed. Raising the Social Security tax base--to pay for the Social Security benefits that already

have been pay for is fraud. I hope lawmakers understand this. Once, the Social Security debt is paid off—then—it may need recalibration.

10. Furthermore, the present plan is fair—based on what you have paid: the Obama's plan is unfair: based on what you have not paid. The big problem: the paid-in S.S. surplus was misappropriated. I agree the U.S. government is in a pickle—they created. And I agree—if, the benefits in the pipeline are not, currently—being funded: that is an additional problem. Cuts in future benefits and higher taxes may be needed. There is no free lunch.

11. I don't see the logic—in skipping the middle class—and applying the S.S. tax on wages over $250,000; when, those making more than $102,000—are better able to pay the Social Security tax—than those making up to $102,000—or under.

12. It seems—by skipping the middle class—and applying the S.S. tax on wages over $250,000: Obama's purpose or intent—is to convert the S.S. plan: from benefits you pay for—to benefits paid by others.

13. Skipping the middle class—and taxing the rich: is a vote getting unjust gimmick: employers are not at fault here. There is one guilty party—one innocent: Obama's plan punishes both.

14. Taxing employers 6.2 percent on wages over $250,000 would be an additional expense—to subsidize retirement benefits for low-income non-employees and for higher retirement benefits for the wealthy—is bad.

15. It is not fair to tax employers—a second time—to pay for what the federal government borrowed from the S.S. Trust Fund.

16. The amount of real assets is the Social Security Trust Funds—zero. The government is supposed to hold the paid-in money; so, that it can pay the benefits when they come due. It has not done that. A big debt has built up--and it now want to get around paying those IOUs—by cutting benefits—or taxing workers a second time. Raising the S.S. tax—to pay off these IOUs—is fraud.

17. Eventually, when the number of people that pay into the S.S. Trust Fund— decreases and the number of people that receive benefits increases: it will be necessary to cut benefits—and/or raise the level of taxation. But, Obama's plan to skip the (upper) middle class—does not make sense.

Maybe, Obama is confusing the Social Security tax with the Medicare tax—it functions on a different principle: it is not based on what you pay in. You qualify; basically, if, you are 65 or older and a US citizen. It is a 2.8 percent tax on wages: half paid by the employee and employer. There is no limit on the amount of wages taxed. Subsidization of medical care—is more justified, than, retirement benefits for seniors. It is a government operated annuity—or pension—based on the tax you paid into the fund. Medical costs are skyrocketing and in many cases unaffordable for the average person. And, sometimes, people are not to blame for their injuries, ill health and diseases.

It cost: $31 billion in 1980.

It cost: $245 billion in 2003.

It cost: $374 billion in 2006.

In 2008, its cost will exceed—what was paid in. One reason: the Medicare prescription drug bill. Its original estimated cost: $400 billion over ten years. It is part D—added to Medicare benefits—it is a colossal taxpayer rip-off. Richard S. Foster, a Medicare director, claims: the Bush administration threatened to fire him, if he disclosed his belief in 2003: the prescription drug bill would cost $500 to $600 billion. More recent estimates: puts the cost at over $1.2 trillion from 2006 to 2016.

These are the words of Senator McCain: "I strongly opposed adding another unfunded entitlement to the fiscal train wreck that is Medicare by providing all seniors with a costly drug benefit, even those, like me who can more than afford to pay for all their medicine."

Barack Obama was not in the U.S. Senate, when this bill was passed (in 2003). His opposition to the bill is the cost of drugs—Medicare should be able to negotiate lower prices (or buy generic drugs)—prohibited by the bill. That is a common complaint. It was designed to enrich drug makers.

For example, Medicare pays $785 for a year's supply of Lipitor and $1,483 for Zocar --used to lower cholesterol levels. The plan pays for 95% of the cost of prescription drugs over $5,100. That is ridiculous, when you consider: more than one-half the people of the world: earn less than $2 per day—or $730 per year. There is something seriously wrong with U.S. medical system. Health care experts say—there are alternative natural means (i.e., to lowering cholesterol).

I believe—the US government is not spending enough on prevention (or education) and too much on treatment or prescription drug—dependency. It is a co-conspirator with the drug companies.

Prevention (or education) is less—costly.

I question whether many of these drugs are needed—and some may even be harmful. I believe, the entire bill should be repealed--and start over. I agree with Peter G. Peterson author of the book: "Running On Empty": medical care must be rationed.

People should take more responsibility for their health—by making life-style changes.

And, I don't believe—the solution to the Social Security future crisis: is to by-pass the

FICA-SS tax on incomes from \$102,000 to \$250,000—and applied to income (or wages) over that amount. That is misplaced anger. A gradual increase in the S.S. tax base, after the Social Security Trust Fund has been restored: plus benefits cuts if deemed unfunded--is fairer. This is proof—Obama has not done his homework on this issue—and is not ready to be president.

But, I don't believe McCain is qualified either. He voted for a 2 year extension of the dividend and capital gains tax cuts (during the Iraq War).

I would like both: the republican and democratic presidential nominees: to be put in the Hot Seat and asked: whether they will continue to raid the Social Security Trust Fund—to operate the federal government—and give the American people a bogus---budget deficit (or surplus)—like Bush Jr.

In conclusion: if, Obama's plan is enacted, the government will be required to pay higher Social Security retirement benefits to millionaires and billionaires—which means: he is an idiot—or totally wrong on this issue!

HR 4297—ONE OF CONGRESS'S MOST SHAMEFUL ACTS

(revised)

The Bush White House: claims: HR 4297 -- The Tax Increase Prevention and Reconciliation Act of 2005—signed by the president: "A victory for American taxpayers." He is a plutocrat and bamboozler. His website states: **In the Past Five Years, the President's Tax Relief Has Helped Spur Growth by Keeping \$880 billion in the Pockets of American Taxpayers.**

What he does not state: ninety percent of those tax cuts go in the pockets of those earning over \$100,000 per year and he added \$2.6 trillion to the Federal Debt.

And it states: these tax cuts Reach Families and Businesses alike. It states: 57 million in all—have some investments in the stock market.

But, the truth of the matter, the richest 10 percent own 85 percent of all stocks.

The Bush White House website also claims: **The President's tax cuts on dividends and capital gains have succeeded in lowering the Cost of Capital and encouraging Businesses to expand and hire New Workers.** That is wrong for a number of reasons. The Fed Funds rate has risen since the enactment of the 2003 tax cuts to 2006: from 1 percent to 5 percent. What may have helped businesses to expand: the reduction of the Fed Funds rate to 1 percent in 2003.

Secondly, it is not a tax cut on businesses--but, on wealthy individuals. HR 4297—contains a 2 year extension of the capital gains and dividend tax cuts. The Bush website—makes a false claim: to justify extending the 15 percent tax on dividends and capital gains to the year 2011.

Inserted into the bill: a $5.1 billion tax break for oil companies—deleted from the bill: tuition deductibility for middle-class people. It also contains a provision: allowing for higher income taxpayers to transfer: IRAs to Roth IRAs, which allows tax-free withdrawals of capital gains, dividends, and interest: 99.7 percent of the benefit goes to the top quintile of income. It also raises the deduction of income subject to the Alternative Minimum Tax.

The prudent thing to do—increase taxes during wars and deficits.

The bill was sponsored by Charles E. Grassley (R), the main stated purpose: help the economy grow and create jobs. This is hooey. I got this word from President Harry Truman. It is a false argument to cut taxes on the wealthy. In 2001: it was the surplus—in 2003: the deficit.

Bill Frist, Senate Majority Leader, reaction to the Bill, said: "We will keep taxes low so that we that we can keep this great country of ours strong and growing". What a phony bastard: this is a tax cut for the wealthiest Americans like himself—its effect is just the opposite.

Senator McCain.com. stated: "As President of the United States I will always put my country first, I want to promise you that. You can count on me because it is what I have done my entire life." That is a lot of hooey, also. He was one of the Keating Five and his voting record and flip-lops—do not substantial that claim; most notably, he voted for HR 4297.

He is a truth-twister—like Bush, First, Grassley, and most republicans. Harry Reid, senate Minority Leader, said: that the bill "caters to an elite group of wealthy Americans at the expense of the middle class."

Citizens for Tax Justice states: "capital gain and dividend tax cuts offer almost no benefit to middle-income Americans and add to the nation's fiscal problems." Tell me: is this what is best for this country? No.

McCain is a republican plutocrat and often—is wrong. How—can you ignore the evidence—(and your conscience)? Don't you listen to others? Are you serving the Republican Party or the people?

Senator Barack Obama, on the other hand, voted against the bill. That shows good judgment.

Here is what some senators said—when this bill was debated in the Senate: May 11, 2006.

Mr. DODD: "Now we about to add $70 billion to that (i.e., the $8.4 trillion deficit at the time) without paying for it."

"Under this bill, mainstream Americans—the middle 20 percent of income earners—will get an average of $20."

"If you make 10,000 to $20,000, you get $2"…."$30,000 to $40,000, you get $16"….."$50,000 to $75,000 range, it is $110"…."more than $1 million, you get a $41,977 tax break"…."more than $5 million a year on average. They get $82,000…". Then, he says: "How many of those people (146,000) do you think actually need that tax break….."

Mr. AKAKA: "Mr. President, once again, we are faced with a tax package that represents misplaced priorities, and that is not in line with the views of a majority of Americans, including taxpayers in my State of Hawaii. My constituents are calling for fairness in tax treatment, and they are not getting it in this package."

Mrs. FEINSTEIN: "I believe this conference report reflects misplaced priorities. It exacerbates an already serious deficit. It certainly exacerbates the national debt. And most importantly, it is certainly not equitable."

She describes the bill--as: "short term gain, long-term pain."

Mrs. BOXER: "We are giving the American people more deficits. We are giving them more debt. We are not helping middle-class families solve the problems of the raging costs of college tuition and the raging cost of gas prices. I hope we vote no on this bill. It is a bad bill."

Mr. HARKIN: "This reconciliation bill gives $70 billion that we do not have, overwhelmingly to people who don't need it; and it passes the resulting debt to people who haven't even been born yet. This bill is reckless. It is irresponsible. And it is shameful."

Mr. KERRY: "Mr. President, today we are debating a $70 billion tax reconciliation bill and the centerpiece of this bill is a provision to extend the lower tax rates on capital gains and dividends that do not expire until the end of 2008. I cannot support this bill for many reasons. It abuses the budget reconciliation process in order to provide and extension of tax cuts to those with incomes above a million dollars rather than addressing tax issues in a fiscally responsible matter."

Mr. OBAMA: "Mr. President, I rise today to speak in opposition to the tax reconciliation conference report.

The Federal Government is the rare institution that can spend money it just doesn't have. We spend and we spend and when we don't take in enough to cover the bill, we just borrow from China and Japan and keep on spending."

Mr. KENNEDY: "The audacity of the Bush Administration and their congressional allies truly knows no limit. First, the Republican majority cuts spending on Medicaid and other important Government programs for people in need by nearly $40 billion. They claim we have to do it to reduce the deficit. Then they bring this outrageous tax bill to the floor, a bill that will cut taxes by far more than the savings in spending from the programs cuts. The net result will be substantial increase in the budget deficit—exactly the opposite of what the reconciliation process is supposed to accomplish. Billions of dollars will go from programs that assist low-income families and senior citizens into the pockets of the already wealthy. It takes from those with the least and gives to those with the most. It is a breathtaking Republican scam on the Nation that can only further discredit this Congress in the eyes of the people.

Mr. DAYTON. "Mr. President, this bill should be a billboard for the corruption of the public interest in Washington. It is a disgrace, it is an abomination, and it should be rejected by the Senate."

Mrs. MURRY: "We need a tax system that is fiscally responsible, helps business grow, and provides maximum relief to the middle class, but this bill achieves none of this. Instead it takes out a loan against our children's future and adds to the deficit. This tax bill makes it more difficult for us to address other important priorities like homeland security, paying for the war in Iraq, our nation's infrastructure, health care, and education. This is the wrong tax plan, at the wrong time, for the wrong reasons."

Mr. SARBANES: "Mr. President we have before us more and more of the same --tax reconciliation legislation that further undermines our underlying fiscal health while providing extraordinary, generous benefits for the very wealthy but little relief for hard-working, hard-pressed, middle-class Americans. As an editorial in today's New York Times says pointedly, 'There's nothing in it for most Americans, and yet all Americans will pay its cost...'

"The Republican conferees who produced this conference report made a series of critical choices. Rather than providing tax relief for millions of middle-class Americans, they have given most of the $70 billion to the wealthy few.

"Rather than extending critical tax provisions that expired at the end of last year—like the research and development tax credit, the college tuition deduction, and the credit for teachers who use their own money for classroom expenses—they have extended tax cuts for the wealthy, which do not expire until 2009. Rather than finding ways to help Americans address the tremendous prices at the gas pumps, they have allowed the big oil companies to continue enjoying their large tax breaks and Government giveaways. Rather than charting a course to fiscal responsibility a change in direction long overdue they have presented us with a bill whose $70 billion in tax cuts will only add to the already-massive Federal deficit, and whose budgetary gimmicks will cost the country billions of additional dollars in the years to come. Among the most egregious of the gimmicks is the provision allowing wealthy taxpayers to contribute more to their Roth retirement accounts. While it provides revenue at this time to offset the costs of the bill's other tax cuts for the wealthy in the near term, it will cost billions and billions of dollars in lost revenue in the future, and this cost will be borne by future generations of working Americans.

"And editorial in this morning's Washington Post sums up this legislation succinctly: 'Budgetary dishonestly, distributional unfairness, fiscal irresponsibility,' adding 'by now the words are so familiar, it can be hard to appreciate how damaging this fiscal course will be.'"

Mr. REED: "Make no mistake, this tax cut will be paid for by borrowing and adding to the long-run structural budget deficit, and it will depress the growth in the American standard of living."

Mr. BINGAMAN: "Let me conclude by saying that there are many reasons why people should vote against this bill. It is bad fiscal policy. It is bad priorities as far as what extensions we ought to be focused on at this time, if we can afford extensions. It also has in it some of these provisions that are bad policy and egregious in the effect they have. I hope my colleagues will reject the bill when it does come to final vote."

The vote in the Senate: 54 yeas -- 44 nays.

Now—who told the truth: those for the bill—or those against? The main argument for the bill: economic growth and job creation (i.e., by cutting taxes on the wealthiest Americans). The average taxpayer will get little or nothing.

This is July, 2008:

The Dow is down 22.5 % since its October high.

The price of gas is in the $4 to $5 range.

There has been a large increase in the number of home foreclosures: it quadrupled in California—in the first quarter of 2008.

There has been a loss of jobs--6 months in a row.

The federal deficit has climbed to $9.5 trillion.

Economic growth has slowed—to a trickle. Three-quarters of people polled: think we are in a recession.

Professor James Edward Maule states: "The games played by Congress with the budget and tax revenues make the NFL's capologists look like amateurs. Whether it's 'robbing Peter to pay Paul' or a matter of smoke and mirrors doesn't matter. What matters is that the practice of hoodwinking people continues unabated. It's a sad reflection on the shortcomings of modern American politics and the culture that tolerates and enables these practices."

Since, it is crystal-clear: this is an irresponsible, pernicious, shameful, and corrupt piece of legislation: those senators that voted for it: should be tried for malfeasance and sentenced to 2 years hard labor.

And one thing more: The White House website states: President George W. Bush "put the death tax on the road to extinction."

For that: I think—he should be tried for attempting to transform the American democracy into a nation ruled by dynastic wealth and power and giving the Death Sentence. I am pissed-off.

MORE ON OBAMA ON TAXES

(revised)

He claims to be the candidate of change: I don't see it, in that, he has over promised what he can deliver—typical of politicians. Between him and McCain: he is the biggest panderer (i.e., to get votes).

Another middle class tax cut is not warranted—right now--the middle class is not paying their fair share; for example (in 2003), those having adjusted gross income of $40,000 to $50,000: paid only on average 8 percent, $50,000 to $75,000: paid 9 percent—and $75,000 to $100,000--10 percent. The reason: numerous tax deductions, exemptions, and credits.

Obama wants to add to the number: giving single taxpayer up to $500 and families up to $1,000 earning up to $75,000—(i.e., to offset the payroll tax). That would add another 10 million people to the 58 million wage earners who pay no federal income tax. That is violation of the basic principle of government--the Head Tax.

It is not fair for the rich—or the top quintile of earners: to pay the Head Tax for 68 million people and their families. That is Obama's tax plan. He has the wrong perspective—on a number of issues.

He wants to impose the payroll tax on all wages from bottom to top, except between $110,000 and $250,000: that is a sign: of missing brain neurons: it does not make sense.

He is trying to get votes: by promising too much.

He wants to give senior citizens a free-ride up to $50,000: that is plain nuts. That would add another 7 million people who pay no income tax and make those that pay—a minority. His tax cuts and credits are destroying the tax base that supports the U.S. government. The average life expecting in the U.S. 78 years: that means retired seniors citizens would pay no federal income tax with on income up to $50,000 for 13 years on average. Right now, there are 36.3 million senior citizens and that number is expected to double by 2030. This is an irresponsible-ridiculous plan. Everybody, who receives benefits from the federal government, must pay their fair share (including senior citizens).

When, you add the other Obama's tax credits, such as: the mortgage interest tax credit for non-itemizers, the retirement savers tax credit, the American opportunity tax credit, and the expanded child and child and dependent care and earner income tax credits—that will further increase the number of people that the government supports—and decrease the number of people that supports the government. Bush cut taxes at the top—Obama is destroying the bottom of the tax base—and adding to the number of people that pay no tax—and get a tax refund. He is taking money from the US Treasury to buy votes from the lower and middle class. These tax cuts and credits are ill-timed, pernicious, irresponsible, and will add to the already towering National Debt—that is depressing the economy.

What is needed: is less deductions and credits and more tax increases from bottom to top, but, mostly at the top—to reduce the deficit

Obama wants to leave the Bush tax cuts in place—except for couples making over $250,000 and single filers $200,000 and more. That is good; but, does not go far enough. Considering the economic mess we are in now: all 2001 and 2003 Bush income, capital gains, dividend, and estate tax cuts—should be repealed. They were based on overly optimistic forecasts and congress failed to reassess the situation after deficits appeared and the Iraq War started—and increase taxes

He espoused--pay-as-you-go--during the campaign; but, his tax cuts and social programs would violate that principle—and increase the already—colossal deficit. He is being unrealistic and dishonest. The Tax Policy Center estimates his tax proposals would increase the national debt up to $3.4 trillion over 10 years.

I am not sure-- you can be elected in America—if, you tell the people the truth. You have to delude the people—to get votes: Bush did it in 2000 and 2004.

The good news: Obama has a good voting record—since, becoming a senator in 2005. Rated 100% by the CTJ

Posted 7/29/08

MORE ON MCCAIN ON TAXES

McCain's mantra: cutting taxes—creates jobs. Not, true—if it swells the deficit. Cutting taxes—(i.e., on the wealthy) is not a guarantee: jobs will be created: there are over powering factors to be considered, such as: the outcome of the Iraq War, the trade deficit, international competition, the war on terrorism, the price of a barrel of oil, etc. He is a bamboozler—like Bush.

His recent vow to balance the budget in four years—without raising taxes: is sign of insanity. It is a vow: he cannot achieve—and it shows desperation. He is trying to out do Obama's promises.

He told a crowd: Obama would raise taxes and "destroy jobs across the country". He is a trust-twister: What he is implying: your taxes. The Obama tax increases are on the top 2 or 3 percent of taxpayers. The Bush tax cuts: have contributed to a loss of 79,000 jobs in June—the worst in nearly 6 years. It helped create a $9.5 trillion deficit to date—that weakened the dollar and the economy. The interest on the National Debt to July--$377,265,344,758 –for which the taxpayers get nothing—over 40 percent goes to foreign countries: cutting taxes to increase government revenues—can be compared to the practice—of blood-letting.

A graduating increase on those most able to pay—to reduce the deficit: does not destroy jobs. It strengthened the economy.

I am not going to give him credit for voting against Bush's 2001--$1.35 trillion tax cut and Bush's 2003--$330 billion Bush tax cut (highly skewed towards the wealthiest taxpayers); because, now, he want to make them--permanent. The size of the present growing Federal deficit makes his position—untenable and irrational. More tax cuts is not the solution.

He has learnt—nothing from the Bush tax cuts; mostly on rich, to create jobs: they created a monster National Debt.

McCain says: "I will….propose---a middle-class tax cut—a phase-out of the Alternative Minimum Tax to save more than 25 million middle-class families as much as $2,000 in a single year."

He is a politico-conman—and nuts.

The middle class—now pays only about 8 to 10 percent on average of their AGI—of $40,000 to $100,000. They are presently under taxed. That would add another: $50 billion to the deficit.

The AMT is essential—to prevent upper income taxpayers from paying little or no tax. It does not affect the middle class. It affects mostly the top 10 percent: earning more than $103,000.

The Tax Policy Center estimates McCain's tax proposals would increase the national debt as much as $5 trillion over 10 years.

He is not being realistic or honest.

In 1999, he voted YES on Social Security Lockbox. I would like to know, as the republican candidate for presidential: does he still think the same way: that would throw a monkey wrench into his balance the budget plan.

He has a mixed voting record (on taxes), since, becoming a senator in 1986, rated 50% by the CTJ.

After, deducting his good vote reversals—I would give him a zero: a totally bad record—since 2001.

PANDERING

(revised)

One reason for our National Debt—and badly designed Tax Code: political candidates running for office—promising—benefits and tax cuts to get elected.

Besides, changing the tax rates and brackets—to reduce taxes: there are two other means: adding to the number of above and below the line deductions, exclusions, and credits (and increasing the amounts).

Above the line deductions reduce gross income to arrive at AGI—a base line for making other tax calculations. Then, there are below the line deductions to arrive at taxable income—one can take the standard deduction—or itemize. Your tax bill: is computed—by applying the tax rates on income within the brackets—after all above and below the line deductions. Tax liability is further reduced by tax credits. For example, in 2003, the average tax paid as a percentage of adjusted gross income of $22,000 to $24,999: 6 percent. That is even lower the 10% tax rate on income from $0 to $8,025 per person. The reason: deductions and credits.

Lawmakers keep adding to the list of deductions and credits—that reduces one's tax bill and undermines the statutory income tax rates and increase the number of filers-- that pay no federal income tax: about 43.4 million in 2004. This is repeated almost in every congress or election—in recent times. Those that propose tax increases, generally, are defeated. These tax cuts, deductions, credits, etc—have, even, a more devastating effect on the higher marginal tax rates.

For example in 2003, taxpayers with AGI of $75,000 to $99,999 paid an average-- only 10 percent: deductions and credits--have neutralized the three statutory rates of 15%, 25% and 28% imposed on this level of income

The top 1% in 2006: paid 22.79 % of AGI. Two big reasons: Bush reduced the tax on dividends from 39.6 to 15 percent—and capital gains from 20 to 15 percent. And, the third big reason: the top 1 percent receives a big percentage of their income from capital gains and dividends. Other reasons: deductions and credits. Preferential treatment of income, deductions and credits neutralizes the statutory tax rates applicable on most of their income of 25%, 28%, 33%, and 35%. Their average income in 2006: $1,301,000. The effective rate is less than the statutory rate on income between $32,550 and $78,850: that is a big reduction.

And, at the bottom of the income scale: there are a growing number of people that pay no taxes—and get a tax credit refund. Today, 41 percent of voting age adults pay no federal income tax.

When, will it stop?

In 2008, both Obama and McCain are proposing more tax cuts, deductions, and credits--to get elected.

Obama wants to reduce taxes more on the lower and middle class in the form of a second—redundant: MWP tax credit—that is refundable—along with other tax credits-- and raise taxes only on the top 5 percent; when, you add his other programs: the net result: more people will pay no tax and get a refund—and the National Debt will continue to climb faster than GDP.

Three of his good votes:

He voted No—on increasing the estate tax exemption to $5 million.

He voted No—on repealing the Estate Tax

He voted No—on repealing the AMT.

McCain is worst: he wants to reduce taxes on all brackets, but more so--on the richest Americans (i.e., to get votes and donations). He is pandering—more to the rich. He also has proposed: a $2,500 refundable tax credit for health care insurance. That will result in even a greater deficit over the next 10 years—according to the Tax Policy Center. This estimate does not include—tax savings that might occur from his plan to cut down on earmarks.

Three of his bad votes:

He voted Yes—on increasing the Estate Tax exemption to $5 million.

He voted Yes--to repeal the AMT.

He voted Yes--to repeal the Estate tax--derogatorily called: the Death Tax.

These three votes would enrich—the richest—and increase the deficit. It is the agenda of the Republican Party.

Today—2008-- we are facing the reality of the Bush tax cuts and it is not what he imagined—or projected. By the time he leaves office: the National Debt will be $4 trillion more than when he took office. And, his tax policies are like a supertanker: it takes time to stop (end the deficits).

The people are going to be sick—when they hear the cost of the interest on the National Debt for 2008, 2009, 2010, etc.

CLEANING HOUSE
ON ITEMIZED DEDUCTIONS

(revised)

There has been a rapid growth in itemized deductions: from 1950 to 2004: from $9.9 billion to $1,081.4 billion. That is high, even; when, you figure in the increase of filers and income. If, you want to make the Tax Code simple and fairer, here is a good place to start.

I would eliminate frivolous and unjustified personal deductions; especially, those that required keeping receipts, etc. That is time consuming and burdensome—and it opens the door to cheating.

The recent scandal of U.K. lawmakers making house expense claims, such as: porn, wine racks, piano tuning, a massage chair, maid, hundreds of sacks of horse manure for gardening, a flat-screen TV, cost of servicing the swimming pool of country home, $450 to fix broken toilet seats over 2 years, $900 for repairing a power mower, $3,000 to clean out a moat on his manorial estate, interest on a mortgage after it was paid off—for 18 months, etc. What is true about UK lawmakers—is true about US lawmakers; but, also true about taxpayers.

Once, you declare—one expense—a fair deduction: it has ripple effect: creating dozens of demands.

Here is a list of some:

Acupuncture

Massages, if recommended by a doctor

Fees paid to practitioner uncertified and unlicensed.

Unpaid loans to friends and family members

Vitamins, if prescribed

Meat diet (as a medical expense)

Organic foods (as a medical expense)

Salt-free diets

Cost of overseas travel for medical or dental work

Cost of installing a swimming pool and maintenance, if recommended by a doctor

Moving family pet expenses

Viagra, if prescribed

Bus, taxi, train or car expense to pick up prescription

State and local taxes:

Admissions

Auto registrations

Beverages

Cigarettes

Cosmetics

Driver's license fees

Excise

Liquors

Tobacco, etc.

OTHER category:

Drug treatment programs*

Cost of alcoholism programs*

Cost of stop smoking programs*

Weight loss programs*

*Note: why should a person get tax deduction—if, the program fails to achieve results? I say: there should be limits—on cost and times (repeated): reduce 50 percent the second time—third: denial.

Interest:

Mortgage interest on second (or vacation) home (if, not eliminate--reduced by 50 percent). I don't believe interest on a yacht or airplane mortgage—for pleasure—is a necessary expense—or justifiable tax deduction.

The Big One:

The $250,000/500,000 capital gains house exemption: too generous: the length of residency requirements—and the rules of repeat usage. It probably—should be a one-time tax exemption: that requires at least 5 to ten years of residency. It should not favor—for investment purposes. And, there should be no exemption, if, the capital gains tax is under 20 percent.

The new rule: you, get the capital gains exemption--even—if—your home was used for business: 25%, 50% or 90%: that is wrong. That favors the taxpayers—and disfavors   the government.

State and local incomes taxes:

They do not pay for federal government expenses: I would put them in the 50-50 justified and not justified—class. It is an illusory tax-break. If, deducted: the federal government loses revenue—and it must make up the difference—by raising other taxes. If, you don't deduct; theoretically, it could lower other taxes.

It is a tax-break—that is justified; if, the government has an annual revenue surplus. That is not the US—state of affairs.

The tax code also has quirks—like, you cannot deduct car, taxi, and bus expenses—to get to and from work—but, you can to pick up prescriptions and you can, if you travel between your home office—and your employer's.

Tax deduction—should be limited—to necessary things—i.e., for the individuals survival. Unnecessary--deprives the government of necessary revenue. It all depends on whether, the person or the government needs it most. That is something: lawmakers must deicide. US lawmakers—have decided: in favor of the individuals—by the unpaid accumulation of the growing National Debt.

The only reason, I would agree with deducting state income taxes from federal: some states don't have one. That makes it fairer.

But, it is not only legal deductions; but, the conversion of personal expenses into business—or government expenses—that are bogus.

In 2003: 94 percent of filers: earning from $200,000 to $500,000 itemized—reducing the tax on AGI—to about 17.5 percent. That is down from 34.47 percent in 1980. And, EGTTRA (2001) made it worst. Hidden in this bill, there is a provision: to phase-out the limitation on itemized and personal deductions for high incomes—by 2010. Nearly, 98 percent of these two tax cuts will go to households with incomes over $200,000—according to the Urban-Brookings Tax Policy Center. The center also states: 65.6 million, out of a total of 151 million taxpayers, pay zero income tax or receive government handouts. That number has been growing: from 17.9% of filers in 1984 to 43% in 2008. Robertson Williams, a senior member, says: "You've got a larger and larger share of people paying less and less for the services provided by the federal government."

The US Government is supporting more people—and less people are supporting the government—more people are getting refunds and paying no income tax, and the top earners are earning more and paying less taxes--creating a rapidly growing Meta-Monster National Debt.

In 2008:

- The top 1% paid an average tax rate of 22.79% on AGI

- The top 6-10% paid 12.60%

- The top 26 to 50 % paid: 7.01%

- The bottom 50% paid: 3.01%

- These average tax rates paid are far below the statutory rates: the reason: tax deductions, income deferrals, tax credits, etc.

This adverse trend—can be corrected—a number of ways:

1. By more extensive auditing of tax returns. It appears, even the most esteemed, will cheat, if you don't or can't look.

2. Clean house on allowable deductions

3. Combine—e.g., the 2008 $5,450 standard deduction and $3,500 personal exemption: into one: $8,950 tax-free income: both have the same effect. That

would make it harder to itemize and create more federal revenue—or increase the tax-free income to $10,000--as an offset: for less allowable deductions. That would make the tax code—simpler.

4. Be more conservative on adding or increasing tax credits; i.e., dollar-for-dollar reductions of tax liabilities. There are two types: non-refundable and refundable. Obama favors refundable—to get votes.

5. You can raise the income marginal tax rates—to compensation for all the tax credits, deductions, exclusions, etc.

6. Levy an AMT on AGI or adjusted net income. I will expound on that later. The problem: with the present AMT—it is perplexing: the treatment of taxable income and deductions are different from the standard method. It is cumbersome: requiring computing your taxes twice—under different rules—for those creeping into the AMT zone--and it mostly affects the top 10 percent of filers and only has two tax rates: not progressive above $175,000.

Posted 8/11/08

REALITY-CHECK!

The total cost of interest on the National Debt—during Bush's time in office to July, 2008, a whopping: $2.896 trillion--for which taxpayers get nothing. And, a good chunk of it is--paid to foreign countries.

At the end of 2007: foreign holdings of Federal Government T-Bills and T-Bonds: totaled 46 percent.

It might be better—to paid for higher taxes now—for a better future, than pay less taxes now—for a bigger National Debt.

THE BIG-BAD CHANGE

(revised)

Prior to May 7, 1997, the tax code allowed a capital gain exclusion of $125,000 from the sale of your home, if you met three conditions:

1. you were 55 years or older

2. lived in the home 3 out of 5 years—prior to the sale

3. it was a first time use of the tax break

Prior to May 7, 1997: the capital gains tax was 28 percent. Then, that was a legitimate tax break for home buyers.

However, the rules were changed in the Tax Relief Act of 1997. The lowering of the capital gains to 20 percent—made the tax break less justified; but also, the age requirement was deleted, the capital gains exclusion was raised to $250,000 for singles filers, $500,000 for joint filers, it required only 2 years of residence out of five, and you get the capital gains tax break—again and again. It converted the motive for buying a house to live in—to buying a house—for investment purposes. The Bush lowering of the capital gains tax to 15 percent in 2003—made the home buyers tax-break—even, less justified. On top of this: there is a tax deduction on mortgage interest. That made house buying for primary residency and investment purposes--very attractive. The 2 years residency requirement out of 5—definitely, favored: house buying for investment purposes. This was bad for people who wanted to buy a house to live in—because, investors who bought, mainly, for a tax-free capital gain--drove prices up. To keep the housing buying market on a roll: teaser loans and ARMs were offered to unqualified home buyers—based on inflated house appraisals. People could not resist—the lure. Eventually, the housing boom that started in the late 1990s, receded in 2000, and took off again in 2001--went bust in 2007. Homes foreclosures rose 79 percent and prices plummeted. The bailout of Freddie Mac and Fannie Mae—chartered to buy up alt-A and subprime home mortgages—from mortgage lenders—securitized, sell and guarantee them--could cost the taxpayers up to $300 billion. The Bush Administration's policies of blocking the states' power to curb predatory lending and encouraging subprime home financing—to grow the economy—and justify his tax cuts on the wealthy—backfired. His "ownership society"—based on deregulation and using tax-breaks, ARMs, and ninja loans to sell over priced houses to unqualified buyers—ended in subprime mortgage meltdown. The number of houses that went into foreclosure in 2007: 1.3 million and in 2008—to July: 414,000.

Housing tax-breaks—should be aimed at people who want to buy a house to live in—not for investors, who want to buy, sell, make a tax-free capital gain—and buy again—or multiple houses: live in 2 years, rent for three, sell and get the tax –break every two years. A $10,000 per year capital gains exclusion up to $100,000 per person—(double for couples) for a primary residency—minimum live-in requirement: 5 years: the unused portion good for second house. That house buying tax-break: meets those requirements. The present Tax Code does not. No—tax break—if the capital gains tax is under 22.5%--based on today's National Debt.

Posted: 8/25/08

THE CALIFORNIA BUDGET CRISIS UPDATE

(revised)

The California 2009 budget deficit is now pegged at $15.2 billion. Two bills have been introduced to raise taxes on the higher income—Californians: both blocked by Republicans. They prefer to layoff government workers, cut services to the poor, and raise other taxes.

Assembly Bill 2372 (Coto) would raise taxes 1 percent on individuals earning more that $1 million.

Assembly bill 2897 (Hancock) would impose a new 10 percent tax rate for those earning more than $136,115 and 11 percent for those earning more than $272,230 per year.

The second is better—than the first.

Reason one: the present California income tax stops being progressive on individuals earning over $44,814 placing the cost of government: more heavily on the bottom and lower middle class.

Reason two: the average AGI of the top 1 percent increased 108.4 percent between 1995 and 2006: the top fifth: 44.9 percent; whereas, the bottom, second, middle and fourth fifth: increased an average of 9.25 percent.

Reason three: since, Schwarzenegger became governor: the cost of government has increased 39 percent—and the state's debt has increased—and the cost of servicing that debt has increased. Therefore, taxes must be raised on those who can afford it most—not the least.

What is wrong: it takes two-thirds majority—to raise taxes in California. That is antidemocratic. It makes it possible—for a minority—in this case, Republicans, to block tax increases on the rich, the most able to pay. This has becomes an obstacle in passing a state budgets.

The governor's reaction to the current budget impasse: sign an order to lay off 20,000 part-time state workers. That shows he is a real-life deranged terminator. It is a misuse—of executive power. He is not having any trouble paying for bills; but he is responsible for the state's deficit. Why punished the lowest people on the totem pole for the bad policies of the people on top: the California legislature and governor.

Gray Davis—response, as State Comptroller, was more intelligent and fair: withholding pay checks from all state elected officials—including himself—until the governor and legislature passed overdue budgets.

Schwarzenegger used his movie star-power—to deceive Californians--by crushing the increase in the car license tax—to get votes. The state has lost nearly $4 billion every year. His solution: sell bonds, instead to close the budget gap—make matters worst—long-term.

What has happened to the federal government---has happened in California: the plutocrats—have seized power.

In 1995, the California income tax had eight brackets. But, during Pete Wilson's two terms in office: the top bracket of 11 percent over $219,872 and the 10 percent over $109,936 were eliminated. He is no different than Reagan. This was wrong; because—there was a large increase in the number of Californians earning higher income--during the nineties. That justified higher marginal rates. Instead—they were reduced. That left the highest bracket of 9.3 percent over $31,700 to shoulder the cost of California's government.

Here is how the super-majority required to raise taxes in California--works against the people: the legislature can cut taxes on the rich—with a simple majority; but, cannot raise taxes except by a 2/3rds majority.

The people were deceived into thinking: it would protect them. It did not. It protected the wealthy.

For example, when Democratic Gray Davis was governor: he preferred to raise taxes on higher income tax brackets—but, could not—because, it would required Republicans to vote for it—to get the 2/3rds majority. The other solution: raise the car licensing tax—that passed.

The people's recall of Governor Gray Davis and the election of Arnold Schwarzenegger was jumping from a hot kettle of water into a cool one—that soon began to boil.

They were fooled.

Repealing the car license tax increase—and borrowing money—to close the state budget gap—was a worst solution. Sometimes—misinformed, angry people—make the wrong decision.

They voted another plutocrat-dumbbell into office: based on his movie star image: he is an actor-governor. Not bad in some respects; but, he is against raising taxes on the rich.

He claims the state cannot continue to burden the rich—people like himself. He favors a 1 percent increase in the sales tax: from 7.25 to 8.25 statewide. It would be higher in Los Angeles County. He is a not a bargain, even at $1. He does not need it: most of his income comes from capital gains and cashing in on his fame—as governor --from residuals from DVDs, TV movie reruns, and video games royalties. One of his business deals reveals how the super-wealthy—shelter income from state and federal taxation: he bought a 474 jet from Singapore Airlines and leased it back: income from the lease is written off as a depreciation expense and at the same time: reduces his investment below market value--and at the end: hopes to sells the plane and pay a low capital gains tax. It is a scheme—without labor, without creating jobs or tangible goods--to make a profit (i.e., out of thin air); using mostly borrowed money—and pay as little tax as possible. Also, he entered into a complex-tax reimbursement scheme between Oak Productions, a front for a corporation he controls, and the producer of Terminator 3—that reimburses him for taxes that might be paid or due working in foreign countries. In other words: his business deals are driven by how he can avoid paying taxes. Not wanting to pay taxes in the country that he worked or wanting reimbursement--considering his high compensation—is perverse. He should reveal his annual income and federal and state income taxes paid—since, becoming governor. This will determine, whether he pays his fair share.

During his two terms in office—the cost of state government has risen 39 percent, the state debt has risen and revenues have plummeted. Why, shouldn't he pay more?

The biggest untapped source of income for the state of California—lies in the top 10 percent. They pay too little taxes—compared to their income; especially, at the top. And this reservoir is getting bigger.

Many Californians earn from $100,000 to millions of dollars per year--yet there is no increase on taxes--after: $44,814. Is that fair? If, the state has a budget deficit—who should pay—the rich or poor?

On August 17, 2008, the Democrats' plan to raise the tax on joint filers earning more than $321,000 to 10 percent—and those earning more than $642,000 to 11 percent—was put to a vote in the California Assembly--and it was blocked by a GOP minority: here is the vote:

45 for—30 against. No Republican voted for it.

The reason— it is a fair tax: the AGI of the top 10 percent of Californians increased 57.4 percent between 1995 and 2006: the middle fifth: 8.5 percent. And between 2001 and 2006: 49.5 percent of the growth in AGI was concentrated among those earning $500,000 or more.

Republicans don't see that way. Governor Schwarzenegger has proposed a 1 percent increase in the sales tax. That would place a heavier burden on the lower and middle class. Let's see what happens!

The California fiscal year begins: 1 July—it is now—in its 56th day of budget impasse.

The Republicans—have taken a no tax increase pledge. That is wrong: to make judgments—before facts are known.

What it means: no higher taxes on the rich—regardless of consequences; such as: laying off teachers, cutting health care to the poor, closing state parks, borrowing more money, even, if the state goes bankrupt.

Posted 9/5/08

ROSS PEROT, THE BOSS

Independent candidate Ross Perot, back in 1992, ran for president—mainly, to straighten out the growing federal debt—which he called "a Frankenstein Monster"—then, 4 trillion. And he used half-hour TV infomercials—to build a case for deficit reduction. After, Clinton: that message was ignored. The National debt is now $9.6 trillion and is growing. Reagan and Bush are responsible for most of this: Bush will add $4 trillion in eight years. Both were plutocrats and deceived the American people. And the two candidates: Obama and McCain--based on their plans--will add to the deficit.

Neither—call for sacrifice—neither tell the (whole) truth. Both plan to raid the Social Security Trust Fund—to balance the budget.

Both are deceiving the American people—both are pandering to get votes.

And the mass media owned and controlled by corporations and the super rich are suppressing, distorting, and ignoring the truth.

They want to hang-on to the Bush-tax cuts.

And, the people are to blame—too. Their minds are set on sex and sports (i.e., the majority). They are neglecting their responsibility of--not only voting--but, voting for the right (or best) candidate.

The main reason for the soaring National debt: is the Republican controlled Congress under Bush. Congress failed to make a U-turn when deficits surfaced in 2002. The 2001 $1.35 trillion tax cuts were based on projected surpluses for the next 10 years. Instead of raising taxes, the government borrowed money to pay for government deficit spending.

Then, in 2003 the congress-plus VP Cheney and Pres. Bush enacted an addition $330 billion tax cuts—favoring the rich—after 2 years of deficits--and days after the invasion of Iraq. Instead of raising taxes to pay for the Iraq War, the government borrowed the money.

Now, we have this enormous debt and Obama and McCain will add to that debt. They are deceiving the American public to get votes. Both are making promises--they cannot deliver on; one, more than the other.

John F. Kennedy—said: "ask not what your country can do for you—ask what you can do for your country."

Obama is just the opposite: besides more tax cuts for the poor, middle class, and seniors, he proposes a number of tax cuts and credits, that would increase the number of voting age adults, that pay no federal income tax from 41 to 50 percent. Less people—paying for the cost of government for more people—is the wrong direction. Plus, he proposes a second stimulus package, free or lower college intuition, seven days paid sick leave, premium health care for all–most of it--paid for by others. That is excessive (considering the current National Debt). Deficit reduction—should be the main priority: not more tax credits.

However, the people do have a right to ask for certain basic needs from the government (based on its GDP)—and that it spends their money (taxes)—wisely, but, not to make them equal—that requires evolution, brains, and work. Barrack believes healthcare is a right for every American. It is more like: 50/50. It is not a right, if you won't work, pay what you can afford, and if, you fail to take reasonable responsibility for your health. People who smoke—do not have a right to new lungs.

Barrack is saying: it's your right to expect others to pay for your healthcare—when, you abuse it. He is off-target. Have you noticed—at times: Barrack looks like the face on the cover of Mad.

But, in America—there is a growing gap between the rich and poor. And the rich are earning more—and paying less tax. That has to be corrected. They need to pay more tax. He is partly right.

The aim—should be—the right medium.

McCain—is the opposite of Obama: he wants a small government: meaning: the rich don't want to pay for the basic needs of the population--or the unfortunate, such as, healthcare. His healthcare plan for the uninsured is a $2,500/$5,000 tax credit: knowing congress won't pass it—and won't solve the problem. It is a vote getting trick. He wants more rich-man tax cuts.

Back in 1992, Ross Perot proposed: raising the marginal tax rate from 31 to 33 percent —and he said: if, that does not do the job—then, raise to 35 percent. Well, 35 percent under Bush—did not do it (reduce the deficit). And times have changed: the income at top--has doubled and tripled, especially, for CEOs of large corporations. Therefore, Obama's plan to raise the top bracket to 39.6 percent would better serve deficit reduction--then cutting taxes on the rich more: McCain's plan. That has increased the deficit.

But, the second part of Ross Perot's plan was spending restraints: here, I believe, McCain is stronger—than Obama.

Ross Perot launched a blog in January of 2008—called: the Perot Charts: I believe— they are helpful—in determining what is needed. I believe the most important, shows that between 1965 and 2007 mandatory spending has increased 27% to 52% of the budget. The biggest of these: Social Security, Medicare, and Medicaid benefits and the cost of these three entitlements are growing faster than GDP. And, if these tends—continue—that will bankrupt the US.

And the most important point: Ross Perot makes—is: "The sooner we confront these issues, the better." And I don't think, neither, Obama or McCain are heeding these figures. They are ignoring the facts.

I might add: there was one Perot Chart missing: showing the increase of income of the top 1 percent, .10 percent, and .01 percent—since, 1980--and the decease in percentage of income taxes paid.

This is the Ross Perot paradox: he voted for George W. Bush—the biggest creator of public debt in U.S. history.

The moral of the story: beware of—who you vote for. Both Obama and McCain are snake charmers; one, more than the other.

Posted: 9/ 9/08

OBAMA'S AND MCCAIN'S VP PICK

Obama picks—Senator Joe Biden.
Former President Bill Clinton said at the DNC: "I love him, and so will America." I checked his voting record on tax reform—and it is impeccable. Rated: by CTJ: 100 percent for progressive taxation.

Here are the main ones:
Voted No—on $330 billion tax cuts (2003)
Voted No—on extending the dividend and capital gains tax cuts (2005)
Voted Yes—on $47B for military by repealing capital gains tax cut (2006)
Voted No—on repealing the estate tax (2006)
Voted No—on repealing the AMT (2007)
Voted No—on raising the estate tax exemption to $5M from $1M (2008)
Voted Yes—on increasing tax rate for people earning over $1 million (2008)

McCain picks Governor Sarah Palin.
He said: "She's exactly who I need. She's exactly who this country needs….."

He needs a good looking and charming female vote getter; but, the country does not need a woman with five children and no national and international experience—as vice president. He is putting himself first and country second. That is making a bad mistake

McCain says: she has "good sense."

I checked her voting record: she has none—never held legislative office. She should be quizzed on: how--she would vote on tax reform—compared to the voting record of Senator Biden. Whether, she agrees with McCain, that the Bush tax cuts should be made permanent. That would determine, whether, she has good sense. As vice president, she would have the power to break a senate tie: that is a scary—possibility. It was VP Cheney's vote—that enacted the Bush 2003 $330 billion tax cuts (favoring the wealthy): scarier, she might become president.

Posted 9/16/08

(SOME) RNC—DISTORTIONS

Attack dog #1 — Fred Thompson—misrepresented Obama's position on taxes. He said: "We need a President who understands that you don't make citizens prosperous by making Washington richer, and you don't lift an economic downturn by imposing one of the largest tax increases in American history".

He should have said: we need a President—who understands: that cutting taxes on its citizens, particularly at the top--has contributed to the soaring National debt. And, this debt—is responsible in part—for the downturn.

The present top marginal tax rates are low—compared to World War II, the Korean War, and the Vietnam War.

I guess--he does not know—we are in a war. And that Bush—will leave us with a monstrous National Debt.

He said: "They tell you they are not going to tax your family." No, they're just going to tax "businesses"! And he says: this will raise the cost of groceries, clothing, and gasoline. Actually, (some) profitable corporations are not paying their fair share of taxes. That increases the federal deficit. And, big deficits are one of the main causes of dollar devaluation—or higher prices.

Obama plans—to eliminate corporate tax loopholes and cut taxes on small businesses. Although, in a couple of cases, they place a burden on businesses, that should be place on the self—or federal government.

He also said: "They say they are not going to take any water out of your side of the bucket, just the 'other' side of the bucket! That's their idea of tax reform."

This is an erroneous metaphor. There are six tax brackets. These are like buckets. Obama plans to take—only from the top two buckets. These would be returned to their 1990s level: 36 and 39.6 percent.

Attack dog #2: Rudy Giuliani. He said: "John McCain would lower taxes, so our economy can grow." That is the continuation of the Bush strategy—and it has failed: the national debt grew faster than GDP.

After, eight years: 90 percent are worst off.

When he said: "McCain would lower taxes"--he is implying on you--when, it is mostly on the rich. And when, he said: "(Obama would) tax us more"--implying on you; when, it is on those--earning over $250,000. He has, repeatedly, stated: the bottom 95 percent would not get a tax increase.

This is a distortion—repeatedly used by McCain.

Attack dog #3: Joe Lieberman. He said: contrast: McCain's record with Obama's—on getting important things done—like balancing the budget. I did. Here is what Senator Lieberman said—concerning: HR 4297: extending the dividend and capital gains tax cuts during the Iraq War—two more years; mostly, benefiting the top 1 percent of taxpayers.

Mr. LIEBERMAN: "Mr. President, I rise in opposition to this tax reconciliation conference report. It is a financially bizarre hodgepodge of misplaced priorities, missed opportunities and misguided economics."

McCain voted YES on this bill.

Obama voted NO. He was right

McCain is for the surge in Iraq—but, not willing to pay for it. In June, 2006, he voted: NO—on $47B for military by repealing the capital gains and dividend tax cut. Obama voted YES. So, did Lieberman—on both.

Therefore, Senator Lieberman's support of McCain for president—must be for other reasons (or motives).

McCain—the Big Bamboozler

He said: "my opponent will raise them (taxes)." This is a distortion: he repeatedly uses throughout his campaign. He means—and says: your taxes (at times). Obama has emphatically said: the bottom 95 percent will not receive a tax increase under his plan. I continue to see false McCain TV ads.

He said—at the convention: "My tax cuts will create jobs. His tax increases will eliminate jobs." He can foresee the future—apparently.

I don't think: he has learnt anything from the Bush tax cuts, over 50 percent going to the top 1 percent. There stated purpose--to stimulate the economy and create jobs. What happened: the Department of Labor--just released a report--stating: that the nation has lost 550,000 jobs so far this year—and the unemployment rate has reached a five-year-high. McCain wants to make permanent these tax cuts and cut taxes on the wealthy--more. What was never mentioned at the RNC: the massive National Debt created by Bush tax cuts and the failure of the republican controlled congress to raise taxes to reduce federal budget deficits--seven years in a row--and during the Iraq and Afghanistan wars. When is the government going to act responsibly—and raise taxes on the most able to pay, instead of—lower.

Presently, they are over compensated and under taxed.

For some reason—those that make one million, a hundred million, or a billion -- from the economy (i.e., the national resources of the nation, government services, national defense, and labors of others)--think—they should pay only 15 percent in taxes—and keep 85 percent of the profit—for themselves. That is extreme egotism. That is one reason; why, billionaires are lining up behind McCain: he has vowed not to raise their taxes.

Should McCain—who owns seven houses get more tax cuts; when, millions of people—are losing their one house—to foreclosure.

The reason: he does know—it is embarrassing.

Criticism of the opponent's position on tax issues is fair game—but, not distortions—practiced at the RNC.

Posted 9/17/08

CALIFORNIA BUDGET DEADLOCK—UPDATE

California is now in its 79 days of being without a budget: for the fiscal year: 2008-9. This is a record.

On August 17—Republicans rejected the Democrats' proposal to add two higher income tax brackets.

On September 9: the Democrats rejected a GOP proposal to cut spending for welfare grants, children's healthcare, college financial aid, salaries of in-home care workers, and dozens of other small programs.

Other options being considered:

Borrow against future Lotto winnings.

Raise the sales tax 1 percent—temporarily

Raise the car license fee.

The real cause of the state's budget impasses: the super majority required to raise taxes and pass a budget—contained in Proposition 13.

In the last 20 years: legislatures have passed a budget by the constitutional deadline of June 30—4 times. That is wrong. It worked in favor of the rich. Legislatures removed two higher tax brackets by a simple majority in 1996--and now, it requires a supermajority—to replace.

The present state income tax is very progressive at the bottom; then, stops: there is no progression--from the middle to the top.

Incomes in California have—sharply-- risen at the top; but, the top two marginal tax rates were eliminated.

Democrats tried to correct it—add two higher tax brackets to help resolve the budget deficit--and it was blocked by a minority of Republicans.

California voters—must, if they get a chance in the future--repeal the 2/3rds majority required to raise taxes; if, they want to solve the state's chronic budget deadlocks—and make the tax code fairer.

Meanwhile, until legislatures makes a deal—hospitals, community colleges, day-care centers and other facilities dependent on state funds go without the money they need to operate.

I heard, on the evening new—last night--the legislatures passed a budget. Governor Schwarzenegger—says: he will veto it.

Posted 9/23/08

SARAH PALIN—WHO

ABC's Charles Gibson questioning of Sarah Palin was weak on tax issues. He asked her: three things you'd change in the Bush economic plans.

Her number one answer: reduce taxes. That is the continuation of the Bush economic doctrine (i.e., mostly on the wealthiest Americans)—not a change. And, it has failed—miserably.

The correct answer: raise taxes.

Alaska has a budget surplus—mainly, from oil revenues and royalties. That is not the case with the federal government: it has an estimated $402 billion budget deficit for 2008—and it is higher for 2009.

Her number two answer: control spending. That is what every candidate says —to get votes.

Then, he asked: "Where would you cut?"

Her answer: "We are going to find efficiencies in every department. We have got to."

Let's be honest: that is a dumb answer. You cannot eliminate federal budget deficits by cutting expenses—alone.

I guess--her support of the $400 million bridge to nowhere—is her idea of an efficient use of taxpayer dollars.

I don't trust her intelligence—as VP.

She is an overconfident, semi-dishonest, small town politician, who lacks the qualifications to be the U.S. Vice President.

Posted 9/24/08

BIDEN VS. PALIN

Senator Biden said on the campaign trail--as Fox News.com put it: "Wealthy Americans Must pay more Taxes to show patriotism."

The right wing media--the voice of the ruling plutocracy—was indignant and resentful. They consider the Biden statement--blasphemy.

Biden defended himself on ABC's morning news to Kate Snow—saying: "It's time to be patriotic, Kate. Time to jump in. Time to be part of the deal. Time to help get America out of the rut." That is what he originally said—or meant.

This is absolutely correct. Since Reagan, the wealthy have been under taxed and their income has increased. The wealthiest 1% of Americans earned 22.06% of total AGI in 2006. That is about double from 1970. Before, Reagan: the top income tax rate was 70 percent—today, 35 percent. Dividends were subject to the income tax tables. Today—it has been separated by Bush—and taxed at a flat: 15 percent—for the most part. Likewise, long term capital gains--one of the main sources of income of the wealthy—has been reduced from 28 percent—to 15 percent.

And the second big reason—why this is correct:

The National Debt is $9.6 trillion and growing. It is growing faster--than GDP. That is detrimental to the economy. And, the war in Iraq and Afghanistan and the Bush cuts-- favoring the wealthy—are mostly responsible for this. That must be corrected by spending cuts and higher taxes. Obviously, the bottom 50 percent of taxpayers—who earned only 12.8 percent of all AGI for the same period—can not pay much more.

The average income of the bottom 50 percent: $30,563.

Bush started the 2-3 trillion dollar war in Iraq—and refuses to pay for. He cut taxes, mostly on the wealthy, instead. By the end of 2010 over 50 percent of the Bush tax cuts will go to the top 1 percent.

Therefore, it is time to raise taxes--on the wealthy—those who have received the most benefits—of this nation's productivity—and were under taxes for the last 26 years and saddled us with this enormous debt with their political power and incompetent leadership; particularly, the Bush Administration—which McCain—has vowed to continue: make permanent the Bush tax cuts—and lower.

Sarah Palin told a crowd at Cedar Rapids: "our opponents, they have strange idea about raising taxes. To them, raising taxes—and Joe Biden said it again today—raising taxes is about patriotism. To the rest of American, that's not patriotism, raising taxes. It is a about killing jobs and hurting small business and making things worst." She continued: "This isn't about anyone's patriotism, it's about Barack Obama's poor judgment."

She is absolutely—wrong, got things backwards, and she twisted what Biden said. She is deceitful—lacks depths of knowledge—and it is her: that has poor judgment—and is giving the voters—the wrong message.

Paying taxes, not evading them, and paying your fair share, particular in a time of war—and high budget deficits, is part of being patriotic.

What brothers me most, when she said: "Joe Biden said it again today--raising taxes is about patriotism." That line brought a chorus of boos. She distorted what he said –or meant. And if, the American people hate paying taxes—our Nation is headed for big troubles.

More tax cuts—will, certainly, increase the National Debt. Biden is much smarter. If, paying less taxes—generated more government revenues: that would be a miracle cure-all. Will voters—be deceived?

Posted 9/25/08

MCCAIN—THE IMMORAL TAXPAYER

Biden said--when Bush called for war and tax cuts—Mc Cain said, "it is immoral, immoral, to take a nation to war and not have anybody pay for it." What changed his mind?

He voted to extend the capital gains and dividend tax cuts during the Iraq War—to the year 2011.

He voted No—on $47 billion for the military by repealing the extension of capital gains and dividend tax cuts—back to 2008.

He now—agrees with making Bush tax cuts permanent during the Iraq War: the hidden long-term cost: $2-3 trillion.

Who is he going to tax—to pay for the Iraq and Afghanistan wars: the middle and lower class?

He believes, for some bias and irrational reason; cutting taxes will generate more government revenues. That is the Bush Doctrine.

The Bush Doctrine—has added $4 trillion to the National Debt—in seven years—and more is coming until the Bush tax cuts sunset in 2010—or are modified or repealed.

And, the extension of these tax cuts by congress—will cost $3.8 trillion--from 2009 to 2018. That is national insanity.

The lowest 20 percent would get--zero percent.

The top 1 percent would get: 31 percent.

He is a greedy, immoral, republican party—loyalist. He needs to change his mind--again! And, that is not likely: he is in the top 1 percent. Furthermore, he voted against a bill sponsored by Christopher Dodd--that would have raised the capital gains and dividend tax on people making over $1 million a year: for $16 billion to pay for veterans' healthcare benefits and the improvement of VA hospitals. He is for veteran's benefit—but, not if, he has to pay for it. Dividends and capital gains are two big sources of McCain's income.

That is immoral, immoral (or unpatriotic).......by his own words. He has consistently voted and supported tax cuts on the wealthy—during the Iraq War.

And, favors continuing these tax cuts---even though, the hidden $2-3 trillion cost of the Iraq—will continue for the next 50 years.

He needs to be sent back to Hanoi—for four more years of re-education and labor—rather, than the White House.

Posted 10/1/08

THE CALIFORNIA BUDGET DEAL

After 85 days of impasse—the longest in history—California has a budget. After—a few changes—Governor Schwarzenegger signed it. The good thing: hospitals, state universities, clinics, daycare centers, contract venders, and other services providers—can be paid.

The bad thing---the budget is no good.

It cuts $7.1 billion for programs, such as: schools, transit, healthcare, payments to disabled and poor, Cal State, and other programs.

But it has no corresponding, legitimate revenue producing provisions--to close the remaining gap—of $8.1 billion. Nearly, all provisions to raise that revenue are accounting gimmicks, borrowing, and an illegitimate. The only one: that is praiseworthy: closing the yacht, RV, airplane, and luxury goods--sale tax loophole.

The rest of these phony provisions—will fail to produce the needed revenue—and pushes the problem to next year.

The most irresponsible—provision—puts borrowing of future Lotto winnings—on the November ballot. This is bad in three ways:

One: the legislature dumped their responsibility—to enact a legitimate and fair tax increase—on the people.

Two: borrowing future Lotto winnings—to pay government expenses for the 2008-9 is exactly—the wrong thing to do. It was a provision that Schwarzenegger campaigned for all year. He should reveal—his federal and state tax returns: to determine—if, he is over taxed. In 2003, his gross income: $13.6 million—and paid 14.7 percent in federal taxes and 6.2 percent in state taxes. That is under taxation--legally cheating the state and federal government. A study should be made—how millionaires and billionaires are able to reduce their taxes--so much. The difference between gross income and taxable: credits, deductions, deferrals, etc.

Three: this proposition is designed, so that, if voters reject it: it will trigger a 1 percent sales tax increase. They put the voters' head in a loose. It should trigger—an enactment of higher marginal income tax rates.

That was passed by a majority—of legislatures.

The people should reject this $10 billion lottery-backed bond measure to reduce future deficits. It is borrowing revenues from future years—that has to be paid back with interest. Taxes do not. It is based on an assumption: these Lotto winnings are needed more now— than in the future. That is a risky assumption. It is precisely—the reason: the U.S. economy is in such a mess: the over use of borrowing: private and public.

The legislature gave voters two bad choices—between borrowing and a higher sales tax. That is a particularly, bad option, because, the MTA also plans to put a half-cent sales tax increase on the November ballot—to fund rail, bus, and freeway projects. That would raise the statewide sales tax to 8.75 percent and in LA County to 9.75 percent. They should have been given the same three options as legislators:

1. Borrowing against future Lotto winnings

2. 1 percent increase in the sales tax

3. Two higher state income tax brackets

Instead: they were tricked and trapped between two by legislators. The third option was deleted.

The super-majority rule—did not protect the average taxpayer: it prevented tax raises on the rich; repeatedly, created budget impasses, and resulted in two illegitimate ballot propositions: the $15 billion bond recovery act that put the state deeper in debt and the $10 billion bond—Lotto borrowing act. The later—trapping the taxpayer; if, they reject it—they automatically raise the sales tax. Right now—the bottom 20 percent taxpayers pay a higher percentage of their income on state and local taxes--than the top 1 percent: that makes adding two higher income tax brackets—more just.

The only long-term solution to the California budget deadlocks—and the inability to raise taxes on those most able to pay, such as; Governor Schwarzenegger and others that have high incomes--not that they would be over taxed—but, that they should pay higher marginal tax rates—than, those earning: $44,814—is to frame a ballot initiative to permit a simple majority to raise taxes and pass a budget. And, let the California voters—decide.

For the mean time—the Schwarzenegger subterfuge won the day: this is part of the budget reform—he signed.

Posted 10/10/08

MCCAIN'S AND OBAMA'S HEALTHCARE PLAN ARE FLAWED.

(revised)

McCain's health care plan would offer a refundable tax credit of $2,500 for individuals and $5,000 for married or families. He said: "So, they can go out and purchase their own health care." The problem with that: they might go out and spend it on something else: rent, food, drugs and alcohol, etc. So, that is a foolish plan. And it would increase the number of people that pay no federal income tax—and become a burden to the government—or other taxpayers. And because, of the size of the deficits: that is not likely to pass in congress. It is a vote getting trick—to out match the Obama plan.

His statement Oct: 2008: "We need to have walk-in clinics"—or "more community health centers": I believe is the better solution (i.e., for those that cannot afford health insurance—or medical treatment).

Seventy percent of people—already have some type of healthcare insurance: the problem is those that don't—or cannot afford medical care.

Obama's plan would mandate that employers provide medical insurance or pay into a fund to subsidize low-income families. That is a flawed plan—also. Employers are not responsible for non-employees. It is public or government responsibility. At some point: for those that can't afford health insurance—there has to be government subsidies directly paid to the private sector—or government-run clinics.

The response to RAM's annual free medical clinics set up at the fairgrounds in Wise, Virginia: proves the government is not meeting its responsibility.

If, the government can afford $700 billion to bailout Wall Street banking and investments firms—it can afford to provide--not premium--but, basic affordable health care to low or no income people—and families. Premium healthcare--that you must be able to afford—or pay for. Just like car insurance: there is basic liability, higher liability, and comprehensive. No one plan—fits all.

The best plan—can be determined by testing.

Basically, there are two kinds: for profit and socialized.

Obviously—we do not have the best plan!

For most people—the best plan—is what others pay for.

Unfortunately—not everybody that wants it—deserves it. If, you don't take care of your health—why—should others. Obama—thinks it is a right. Wrong.

Rules, cost, limits, exclusions—must be part of a medical plan.

However, a national health plan—must be mandated. McCain is for voluntary; that, screws up the plan. The rich—would choose not to contribute. The stupid would take a chance of never needing a doctor.

Universal health or medical care is the Ideal Goal.

Posted 11/6/08

WARREN BUFFETT, THE "ORACLE OF OMAHA"

(revised)

Back in February—2008: he told the Toronto Board of Trade: "I am a huge bull on the American economy"--and he said: No economic bailout necessary. Of course, that proved to be false.

And, I might add: the dates of his investments in GE and Goldman Sachs; shows, he was a huge bear, before he was a huge bull.

On October 4, he said on the Charlie Rose show: "We have a terrific economy" that something a big investor would say—i.e., to instill confidence. But, the truth of the matter—it is not so terrific. US economy—can be compared to a giant skyscraper: the first floor: agriculture, two: exploitation of natural resources, three: manufacturing, four: transportation, five: marketing, etc. In one of the rooms near the top—a subprime mortgage meltdown is taking place—or fire—and rapidly spreading to other rooms: auto loans, credit card debt, etc. The financial services are on the 99th floor: on the top floor: sit the CEOs of banks, investment firms, and corporations, which finance and manage the businesses of the nation. Money is the abstract representation—of the physical value. This giant skyscraper, represent the US economy—or Dollar and everything that people do and think—in the US and to a lesser degree—the world--has an impact. Here are some of the reasons why the economy is not—so terrific—or in danger.

I.   The cost of the Afghanistan and Iraq wars; since, 2001: $904 billion and growing.

II.   Between 1994 and 2008—the trade deficit has increased from 1.5% to 4.7% of GDP: $674 billion for 2008.

III.   Total private and public debt—has soared from $11 trillion in 1997 to $53 trillion last year. Principle and interest payments are a big burden—and will hinder future economic growth.

IV.   Credit derivatives have grown from $900 billion in 2000 to $45 trillion in 2007. Warren Buffett called derivatives a "ticking time-bomb." The reason for this: that debt ratio to assets is high and a small change in the market—can result in huge gains and losses. If, there is a major increase in the number non-conforming MBSs or CMOs: the insurer of these securities: will not be able to make good: the credit default swaps—creating huge losses and write downs. What is needed: more oversight and regulation.

V.   **Five pieces of legislation contributed to the home mortgage meltdown:**

1.   The passage of the Community Reinvestment Act in 1977—that encouraged lending to uncreditworthy borrowers and its amendment in 1995—that allowed securitization of these mortgages.

2.   The Depository Institutions Deregulation and Monetary Control Act of 1980: that abolished the states usury cap on mortgages: that gave banks the incentive to make home loans to people with lower credit scores and charge higher interest rates.

3.   The Alternate Mortgage Transactions Parity Act of 1982: that lifted the restrictions barring banks from making anything but the conventional fixed rate, amortizing mortgages--giving birth to risky types: adjustable rate mortgages, balloon payment mortgages, interest rate only mortgages, and Option-ARM.

4.   The repeal of the Glass-Steagall Act by the Gramm-Leach-Bliley Act of 1999. The Glass-Seagall was enacted in 1933—to protect banks from risky investments, to safeguard people's deposits, and limit the risk of the FDIC, which guaranteed these deposits. The act tore down the firewalls between

banks, insurance and securities companies and created giant financial conglomerates, such as: Citigroup, Bear Stearns, Lehman Brothers, AIG, etc. This act—also let these giant financial institutions: composed of banks, insurance, stock brokerage, credit card, hedge fund, and financial service companies to underwrite and trade mortgage backed securities and collateralized debt obligations.

5. The Futures Modernization Act of 2000—exempted derivative transactions—or CDSs from regulation by the SEC or CFTC. Credit Default Swaps insured MBSs and CDOs. Because, derivative contracts were under funded, when the housing bubble burst: financial firms, like AIG FP could not make good the swap. Because, it was too big to fail—the government came to its rescue: taxpayers were not told, initially, TARP (taxpayer) money went to pay off their bad debts worldwide. These bad debts consisted of their inability to make good claims on derivative contracts—or CDSs—or risky bets.

   a. The act included the "Enron Loophole"—exempting energy speculators from US regulation and oversight.

   b. Congress eliminated the "Enron Loophole" attached to a Farm Bill—by over riding Bush's veto in 2008.

   c. The act legalized financial gambling in the dimly lighted world of over-the-counter; i.e., make bets on the future price of stocks, bonds, commodities, SIVs, and other things.

   d. It also made it legal to sell single stock futures in US markets—like commodities: pork bellies, cotton, corn, oil; except, they are not. This is rotten and serves no useful purpose—except gambling.

These five major acts of Congress—essentially—deregulated banking and investment with disastrous results: some went bankrupt, some were sold for pennies on the dollar, and others were bailout by the Federal Government.

VI. Debt has increased as a percentage of GDP from 33% in 1980 to 69.9% in 2008. That means: debt is growing faster than productivity. Last year: the total debt increased $4.5 trillion—5.5 times more than the GDP: that is bad for the economy, and if, that trend continues—it will be disastrous.

VII. Manufacturing has decreased from 29.3% to 12% of GDP--and financial services have increased from 10.9% to 20.4% of GDP—from 1950 to 2005. That means: creating wealth by investment strategies—has over taken creating wealth by the production of tangible goods--creating a structural weakness in the skyscraper. Here are the three biggest sources of wealth-building—that Americans depend on--other than wages and business profits:

    1. The increase of house prices: they tripled from 1995—to 2006.

    2. The increase in stock prices: DJIA rose 10,000 points from its low in 1995—to its high in 2007.

    3. Speculations in derivatives: options, futures, swaps, etc.

VIII. Speculation in derivatives—has become larger, than investments in the stock market—in estimated notional value. For example, Warren Buffett—made over $2 billion from forward contracts: betting US dollars against other currencies. He profited—but, no real wealth was created. His win was somebody else's loss. In other words: capital is being diverted from real productively—to predatory.

IX. The polices of federal government departments and agencies nurtured the subprime mortgage boom/bust. HUD loosened mortgage restriction to permit first-time home buyers with low credit scores to buy a house, who would not have qualified--otherwise; banks were pressured into financing first-time home buyers with poor credit and barring them from making identity and Social Security numbers checks, and the US Treasury Department's Office of the Comptroller of the Currency-- struck down attempts of states to prevent repackaging home mortgages by the secondary market. This led to a tenfold increase in the volume of subprime mortgages--originated from 1994 to 2003.

X. Deregulation resulted in the degradation of lending standards. Homes were sold with little or no down payment—to buyers with lower FICO credit scores: 680 to 575 considered subprime. They were offered low interest rates to get in—that reset higher in 2 or more years. Some mortgages were interest only payments—or had negative amortization. Sometimes credit applications were not documented or verified—as to income, job history, etc. There was also was fraud: credit applications were falsified, house appraisals were inflated, misrepresentation and pressure were used to sell and finance homes.

XI.   Deregulation: permitted banks and mortgages lenders to sell these home mortgages to investment banks—that set up Special Purpose Entities to transform them into MBSs or CMOs--and sold to investors. This process is called—securitization. It shifts the credit risk from mortgage lenders to buyers of MBSs. They are similar to interest bearing bonds. This scheme worked well—as long as--house prices kept going up and borrowers paid their mortgages; unfortunately, that did not happen.

XII.   In 1997, congress changed the tax code--to give home buyers and investors--a tax free capital gain of $250,000 over and over again: to stimulate the housing market —or pump up the bubble.

XIII.   Freddie Mac and Fannie Mae were government sponsored entities designed to meet certain economic and social goals. Mortgage lenders sold their subprime mortgages to Freddie and Fannie—divorcing them from the risk. They securitized and sold them to financial institutions and investors—guaranteed by the FHLMC—the official name of Freddie. HUD mandated that the mortgages they purchased were at least 42% below median income: that target was increased to 50% in 2000 and 52% in 2005. It ending in disaster; when, defaults rapidly increased and home prices fell. In September 2008: both were place in conservatorship: the potential loss for taxpayers—in the hundreds of billions. They hold or guarantee about half of the $12 trillion outstanding residential mortgages.

These two giant quasi-public corporations were wracked with accounting scandals, securities fraud, excessive executive compensation, and illegal campaign contributions.

The CEO of Fannie Mae—received $12.2 million in compensation in 2007—despite a $1.5 billion loss.

The CEO of Freddie Mac—received $19.8 million in compensation in 2007—even though: the company lost half its value.

Shareholders—all, but wiped out.

XIV.   A big part of the home mortgage crisis was mortgages lenders: they are not subject to the same regulations as banks; hence, they became mortgage mills: that sold their toxic originations to the secondary market--for securitization— like, (sick) animals to the slaughtering house—cut up and graded for the market

with very little government oversight. Greenspan said: "it seems superfluous"—
to regulate derivatives.

XV. In 1995, a new derivative was invented: the credit default swap or CDS. They were sold to insure CMOs, MBSs, etc. In case of default: they would be repurchased. The problem: issuers of these credit derivatives did not have sufficient reserves to make good the swap, in the case of, a precipitous rise in defaults.

XVI. To stimulate the stock market—the government lowered the capital gains tax from 28 to 20 to 15 percent. That made the statutory tax on income from investments in securities and real estate--lower than income from businesses and labor---that produce tangible goods.

XVII. Congress created: the IRA and 401K pension plans—to permit (or induced) people to invest into the stock market—to kept prices rising. In 1978, the Internal Revenue Code was changed: to defer taxes on income and earnings in 401K plans until withdrawal. That rapidly increased investments in securities and mutual funds--pumping up the stock market.

XVIII. The tax code—made interest on first, second and third mortgages tax deductible and home owners—over extended themselves. As home prices increased, they took out a second or third mortgage. Then, when prices fell—they ended up with negative equity.

XIX. To keep the economy growing: the consumers were flooded with pre-approved credit card offers—and incessant phone calls: to refinance their house—and take out a cash—or take out a home equity loan—to pay credit card debt—and other purposes.

Bush told the people: go out and spend to grow the economy. They did—but they spent too much or exhausted their savings.

Credit card debt soared to $937.5 billion in 2007--up 7.4 percent from the previous year. That is bad news, because median income rose 1.3 percent. Private debt was increasing faster than income.

Personal savings: that was 10 percent of income in 1982—fell to a negative 1.1 percent in 2006. Consumers were maxed out. "Consumers don't have the buying power any more" –said Mervyns, the retain chain, that recently collapsed due to the current retail slump.

XX.   The economy was slowing in 2008; so, the government passed a $168 billion stimulus package—to get the economy going--again: that was unfunded and added to the National debt.

XXI.   In the US—the few are getting richer—and the middle class and workers are getting less of total income: here are seven indicators:

1. The share of capital income—i.e., from capital gains, dividends, interest, and rents-- earned by the top 1% from 1979 to 2003 has increased from 37.8% to 57.5%—and the share of the bottom 80% has decreased from 23.1% to 12.6%.

2. From 1997 to 2002: the income of the top 1 percent grow 11.3% or $332,800: the lower fifth: 4.5%--or $600.

3. In the economic expansion of 2002 to 2006: the top 1% captured almost ¾ of the income growth.

4. In 2005, the income of the top 1 percent increased 14 percent—or $139,000: the income of the bottom 90 percent dipped 0.6 percent or $172—from 2004.

5. From 1990 to 2007: the pay of CEOs increased 298.2%: the pay of production workers: 4.3%.

6. In 2005, the top tenth of 1% (300,000) people had as much income as the bottom 150 million Americans: nearly double from 1980.

7. In 2005, the top one-hundredth of 1% had an average income of $25.7 million, up nearly $4.4 in one year.

XXII.   There was a sinister side to financialization: the growth of giant predators called: Private Equity and Hedge Funds—that used computer programming, tracking, exclusive information, and market expertise—to beat the markets—and create huge profits—for a few investors. Some became billionaires. That is, basically, legalized financial gambling.

XXIII.   The danger here—this giant skyscraper built upon economic growth, asset appreciation, profits, and the extension of credit: promissory notes, mortgages, credit cards, bonds, credit derivatives, and government borrowing: could implode, one floor upon the other—if, it fails to pay its debts---or if the economy contracts. It needs new girders—or strengthening.

XXIV. During Bush Administration: the national debt ceiling was raised seven times:

7. October 2008 to.... $11.3 trillion

6. July 2008 to......... $10.6 trillion

5   September 2007 to.. $9.815 trillion

4. September 2006 to.. $8.965 trillion

3. November 2004 to... $8.184 trillion

2. May 2003 to .... $7.4 trillion

1. June 2002 to ... .$6.64 trillion

When Bush entered office: the debt ceiling was $5.951 trillion. The bad news is: the national debt has increase faster--than economic growth. That weakens the super structure of the giant skyscraper.

XXV. There was a record breaking deficit in 2008—of $455 billion. That figure is bogus: it does not include off-budget expenses.
    McCain asked Obama in the final presidential debate: "How--why would you want to increase anybody's taxes right now?"
    Here are three reasons:

1. To pay for the Iraq War he supported

2. To pay for the bailout he voted for

3. Seven years in a row of deficits. Duh!

XXVI. In the last 28 years, the monied elite has seized control of the US government by means of political donations, lobbyists, and backing candidates for office: that fulfill their mission: one—cutting their taxes to the bone. I have listed them on my website: posted 4/2/08.

XXVII. From 1950 to 2000 corporations paid an average of 17 percent of federal taxes—now it's down to 7 percent.

XXVIII. When, the housing bubble burst in 2006 and more in 2007—and plummeted in 2008: the stock market—followed on its heels: they are interlinked.

XXIX. The housing and stock—price decline was also intertwined with the economy, deficits, trade imbalance, lower sales and job losses.
Home owners could not make payments on their ARMs—or walked away--as values of their homes dropped and foreclosures—rapidly increased.

XXX. Financial institutions and investors holding large portfolios of MBSs—i.e., mortgage backed securities--suffered huge losses and write downs—as home prices fell: 30% to 50%—and the subprime default rate tripled from 2005 to 16% by October 2007--to 25% by May 2008—and higher in some states.

XXXI. MBSs or CMOs had a risky side—rating agencies overlooked: the opposite of up—as house prices fell—and delinquencies and foreclosures increased: their value sharply dropped and became unmarketable—like junk bonds. In 2007, home mortgages outstanding: totaled $11.2 trillion--$1.3 trillion subprime. Today, about 1 in 6 mortgages are underwater; mostly, subprime--and in this group: the default rate—is rapidly rising.

XXXII. Deregulation of banking—resulted in mortgage lenders making riskier loans, selling the subprime mortgages, and passing the credit risk to others. It is like eliminating the traffic stop signs and speed limits; naturally, there will be more accidents, injuries, and deaths.

XXXIII. In the securitization process: the banks and buyers of MBSs traded places: the banks got their money and the investors got the bank's mortgages: a bad deal, if borrowers fail to pay the P & I.

XXXIV. Deregulation of mortgage lenders: resulted in predatory lending practices: saddling home buyers with mortgages they cannot pay for. Today, 5 million households are behind in payments--and, according to Realty Trac, foreclosures increased 71 percent in the third quarter.

XXXV. There were dire warnings about abusive and risky lending practice in the mortgage markets—back as early as 2000, but Congress failed to pass bills to reform lending practices, regulatory oversight of GSEs, and the secondary mortgage market in 2003, 2004, 2005, 2006, and 2007.

XXXVI. Securitization of subprime home mortgages: shifted the credit risk from banks or mortgages lenders to investment banks—that transformed them into MBSs, rated AAA, and passing the credit risk to financial institutions, such as: pension funds, credit unions, and insurance companies, who bought the bonds. To make them more marketable—they were insured with CDSs.

XXXVII. One reason (subprime) MBSs were rated triple A investment grade securities: rating agencies were paid big fees by the investment banks—that securitized and sold them. They failed to identify evidential structural defects or risks in these financial products: their god—big money.

XXXVIII. Deregulating of banking, the Greenspan Fed attitude, and the failure of the Congress to act: resulted in the origination of $1.8 trillion of these toxic mortgage backed securities, since the year 2000—and sold around the world—like tainted milk—to unwary buyers.

XXXIX. In the securitization process: risky pools of subprime and alt-A mortgages were transformed into top rated investment securities—or bonds—like, lead into gold—and insured by underwriters—without enough reserves: to make good a rapid increase in claims. It was a $1-plus trillion Wall Street—fraud.

XL. Many large investment firms that insured MBSs or CMOs with CDSs—when, the default rate increased and house prices fell--to make good the swaps—had to sell good assets, issue new stock, borrow, or declare bankruptcy.

Uncertainty---bad debts and big losses of the banks and investment firms caused a credit squeeze.

Frightened people begin to withdraw their deposits from banks and thrifts—worsening the situation.

And, the federal government stepped in: to bailout these Wall Street investment firms and banks—laying the cost on the taxpayers and increasing the National Debt. The $700 billion Wall Street bailout—is just the beginning.

The winners from this collapse of the financial house of cards: MBSs, ABSs, CMOs, SPEs, CDSs, SIVs, CDOs, etc. Wall Street executives: Dick Fluld, CEO of Lehman Brothers, made off with $354 million in five years; E. Stanley O'Neill, former CEO of Merrill Lynch—got a $161 million severance package; James E Cayne, CEO of Bear

Stearns—got $131.2 million in five years; Angelo Mozile, CEO of Countrywide—earned $200 million from 2001-6; Joseph Cassano, AIG FP chief executive—make over $280 million in the eight years—prior to its near collapse and rescue by the federal government. Now, you know that this is wrong: multi-million dollar salaries and bonuses and stock options and awards for bad performance.

Executives involved in bringing these tainted financial products to market—should be put in jail and their ill-gotten gains confiscated—of course, that is not likely to happen. It is easier—to charge taxpayers—for their bad debts.

Other reasons why: the economy is not so terrific: there has been a job loss nine months in a rows, sales are down three months in row, corporate profits are down, the cost of living index is higher, house prices continue to fall, economic growth declined in the third quarter, the Dow lost 14.1 percent in October—alone, and the people's confidence level is at its lowest—since, 1967.

The stock market has lost $4 trillion of its value—from its high in October 2007 to September 2008.

And another big reason; why, the US economy is not so terrific—the national debt has risen from $5.9 trillion to over $10.5 trillion during the Bush Administration —so far. This is a tremendous weight on the economy—i.e., interest and principle payments. Tax increases were needed—to balance the budget, but Bush said: that would hurt the economy. He got it backwards. He opted for tax decreases—mostly, on the wealthy, ballooning the National Debt.

Other reasons: the USA was buying more foreign goods and manufacturing less and oil production had peaked: all these factors converging at the same time—has caused the worst economic crisis, since the great depression. It now has to work it way out of this economic mess. And, the National Debt-- will grow for the foreseeable future—because, the Bush tax cuts are still in place until 2011, unless repealed; the economy is deteriorating, and the bailout of the nation's banking and financial system, will add to that debt; regardless, who becomes president. If, you listen to the debates—it is partly, an argument over who will cut or raise taxes—the most. McCain says: he will cut taxes—and Obama will raise taxes. Obama says: the bottom 95 percent will not receive a tax increase. Both are pandering to voters. The truth is--everybody—must pay more taxes—but, more so, the rich, to get out of this mess. It is time to stop the dishonesty.

America—must get back to basics—and create a real economy--based on the production of tangible goods and services--not one, that relies, foremost, on financial services to achieve wealth—or predation. It must take it mind off of sex and sports—and devote more time learning about the issues, what candidates are proposing, and what the congress is doing—and so it can vote intelligently—and see through the distortions. It needs to live within its means. The overweight and obese need to eat less and exercise more to improve their health and reduce medical costs. It needs new, smarter, democratic leadership. It also needs tax reform

Taxing capitals gains—less that than labor—or small business and corporate profits—that produce tangible goods and services—is unfair. It spurred the growth of thousands of hedge funds—that feed on the markets of the world, such as: securities, commodities, currencies, indexes, etc. Trading in the derivatives does not create tangible goods and services. In 1990, the stock market was 6.5 times larger than derivatives. Today— derivatives are almost double the size of the stock market. Some derivatives have a legitimate purpose—but, they also can be used to exploit and destroy--the wealth of others. Buffett also called derivatives: "weapons of financial mass destruction"; but, all derivatives—are not the same. Some are used to protect investments—or minimize risk. Some are just side bets—on outcomes--without owning the underlying assets—or legalized financial gambling.

Derivatives create the false illusion: hedging could prevent disaster from a market decline But, the steep fall in home prices—and mortgage defaults wiped out the equity of many investment firms—and their reserves—needed to compensate buyers. You cannot insure everybody—from a major market decline--somebody has to take the loss. Investment banks—or issuers of derivatives are not subject to the same capital and reserve requirements—as insurance companies. And, the SEC acerbated the problem: by increasing the leverage ratio for investment banks from 12 to 1--to 40 to 1. In 2008, the total credit derivative market has grown to $63 trillion—several times greater than the US GDP. In the event of a severe decline in productivity—or recession: all unsecured, unearned, or phantom wealth would be vaporized. The issuers of credit derivatives: would only be able to pay claims of $1—on $40 owed.

How this ends: will unfold in the future. Some of this loss is psychological—the physical assets are still there. Some of it—is lack of regulation. Some of it is greed. Some of it is misrepresentation. Some of it is over leveraged assets. Some of it is based on realities: job losses, trade deficits, the rapid depletion of natural resources, loss of manufacturing, state and federal debt, the Reagan and Bush tax cuts, etc. It can be turned around—by turning negatives into positives.

A fair tax code is at least, one cornerstone of a good or sound economy. Warren Buffett is also right—on that subject. It is not fair. But, he has not responded to my letter and book. Instead, he has invested $5 billion in Goldman Sachs. The repeal of the estate tax: will cost the government: $750 billion over the next decade. This continues to be a republican goal.

According to my account at iUniverse Publishing Services—as of July 2008, I have sold only 1 copies of my book: "The Estate Tax and Politics", which was published in December of 2006. I believe it contains—information useful in reforming the Tax Code. That letter to Buffett is contained in my book: *Why the Reagan and Bush tax cuts are Unfair* (second edition)."

I am thinking a couple reasons—why he has not responded to my letter and book—that defends the Death Tax: hubris and fear.

One reason: for Mr. Buffett's great wealth: he has never paid capital gains tax on appreciated assets—referring to B.H.

He has donated $31 billion in Berkshire Class B shares to the Bill and Belinda Gates Foundation. The reason: I brought this up: there are two big loopholes in the tax code.

One: Mr. Buffett said: repeal of the estate tax would be a "terrible mistake"; however, this donation is evasion. The question I have: what has the Gates foundation done for him. He owes a big part of his wealth to the United States. That should be his first loyalty.

Two: there is no capital gains tax at death and this donation to the Gates foundation means: no capital gains tax will be paid on his appreciated assets. That cheats the federal government: twice. Therefore, I believe donations to charities of appreciated assets—first: should be taxed for capital gains—and the remainder going to charities.

And there is a third—loophole here: the 2009 estate tax exemption is $3.5 million per person (double for couples). A big percentage—is capital gains: that never will be taxed. That is a loophole. My plan: reduces the exemption, and instead of, one high rate of 45 percent—it reinstates graduating rates. And, I recommend: repealing the 1 year repeal of the estate tax—for 2010. If, not repealed by then: the federal government will lose about $24 billion.

My book: *The Estate Tax and Politics.*-explains why the estate tax should not be repealed—and strengthened. It has run up against a media blockade. Mr. Buffett has the means to break through.

My other book: *Why the Reagan and Bush Tax Cuts are Unfair* (second edition with the 2006 and 2007 updates)—that recommends higher income tax brackets: sold only 2 copies to July of 2008.

Is it not a terrific economy—when, one man's estimated wealth is $62 billion —and 47 million live below the poverty line and cannot afford health care? Tax reform is badly needed.

One big reason: the Federal Government is over $10.6 trillion in debt and is rapidly rising: people, mostly the rich, are under paying their taxes. Therefore—I ask Mr. Buffett: Why don't you like my book? It explains: why, the estate tax is a fair means of collecting back taxes owed. I have given six more reasons why it is a fair tax on my blog: posted 3/18/08.

And I ask this question, because—you are called: the "Oracle of Omaha" and according to Forbes: the world's richest man.

Start with: did you receive my book and did you read it. And what do you think? Silence—at a time like this—is sinister!

THE MEDIA BLOCKADE

I checked my account at iUniverse Publishing Services and to November of 2008—and I sold 4 copies of my book: *Why the Reagan and Bush tax-cuts are Unfair* (second edition)—despite an advertising campaign. First, I send 14 copies of the first edition, published in 2005 and 14 copies of my 2006 updated version: to people in the media: no reviews, no comments, no replies. I was hoping people in the media—would make by message—public. Those people are named in second edition.

I also tried to advertise my books on the Internet: using ad words without success.

When, I published the second edition with the 2006 and 2007 update in October of 2007-- I sent twenty more promotional copies to following people—in the media:

1. David E. Sanger, NY Times

2. Pete Williams, NBC News

3. Jeffrey Birnbaum, Washington Post

4. Charlie Rose

5. Brian Williams, NBC News

6. Senator Harry Reid

7. James Warren, editor of Chicago Tribune

8. Eleanor Cliff, Newsweek

9. David Brancaccio, PBS

10. Hugh Hewitt, Townhall

11. John Harris, Politico

12. Linda Robinson, US News

13. David Ignatius, Washington Post

14. James Kitfield, National Journal

15. John P. Dickerson, Slate Magazine

16. Ed Schultz

17. Tucker Carlson, MSNBC

18. Tony Blankley, The McLaughlin Group

19. Robert Scheer, Truthdig

20. Al Gore

21. I continued to send out letters with the front and back covers of my book or the Frontpage of my new website: thetaxguardian: to about 250 people in the media and government. Here is the list:

Unnamed newspaper editors: The Arizona Daily Star, Albuquerque Journal, The Patriot News, San Jose Mercury News, The Akron Beacon Journal, Seattle Post-Intelligencer, The Grand Rapid Press, Dayton Daily News, The News Tribune, Philadelphia Daily News, Post-Standard, State Columbia, Hartford Courant, Pioneer Press, Richmond Times-Dispatch, Austin American-Statesman, The Tennessean, The Florida Times-Union, The Advocate, The Buffalo News, The New Yorker, The Sun, The Arizona Republic, NY Daily News, San Francisco Chronicle, Long Island Newsday, Sun-Sentinel, The Dallas Morning News, Boston Herald, Tampa Tribune, The Miami Herald, Orlando Sentinel, Chicago Sun-Times, New York Post, Portland Oregonian, Sacramento Bee, St. Petersburg Times, Arkansas Democrat-Gazette, Pittsburg Post-Gazette, Las Vegas Review-Journal, Houston Chronicle, Charlotte Observer, Philadelphia Inquirer

Named newspaper editors: Dennis R. Ryerson, Indianapolis Star; Ken Brusic, Orange County Register; Dave Bundy, St. Louis Post-Dispatch; James A. Hought, Charleston Gazette; Donald Woman, Detroit News; Don Dzwonkowski, Free Press; John Drescher, The News and Observer; Tom Scarritt, Birmingham News; Michael Fancher, Seattle Times; Gregory Moore, Denver Post; Rob Gates, The Sun; Marc L. Davidson, Daytona Beach News-Journal; Frank Scandale, North Jersey Media Group; Bill Osborne, San Diego Union; Julia Wallace, Journal-Constitution; Lewis Bresee, Hartford Courant; Alex Adwan, Tulsa World;

Mark Platte, The Honolulu Advertiser; Christine Mautone, The Journal News; Ron Royhab, The Blade – Toledo; Mike Connelly, Sarasta Herald Tribune; Don Lindley, The News-Journal; Date Darymont, News Press; Frank Scandale, The Record-Hackensack; Eric Alterman, Altercation; Robert W. McChesney, Free Press

Senators: Patty Murray, Jack Reed, Jeff Bingaman, Christopher Dodd, Daniel Akaka, Barbara Boxer, Tom Harkin, Kent Conard, Joe Lieberman, Jay Rockefeller, Robert Byrd, Dick Durbin, Dianne Feinstein, John Kerry, Edward Kennedy

Congressmen: Nancy Pelosi, Dennis Kucinich, Charles Rangel, Sander Levin, Bob Etheridge, Pete Stark, Lloyd Dogget, Jim McDermott, Rahm Emanuel

Others: Allan Sloan, Newsweek; Professor Eleanor W. Brown, Regent University School of Law; John Roberts and Brent H. Baker, News Busters; David Cay Johnson, NY Times; Leo E. Linbeck Jr., Americans for Fair Taxation; Joan Claybrook, Public Citizen; Ralph Nader, Citizen Works; Gerald Prante, The Tax Foundation; Edward Nathan Wolff, New York University; David Moore, The Sunlight Foundation; Tavis Smiley, Arianna Huffington, Tom Gjelten, NPR; Danielle Brian, Taxpayers for Common Sense; Barbara Slavin, USA Today, Bill Moyers, Paul R. Krugman, Princeton University; Craig Brown, Common Dreams; Hamilton Fish, the Nation Institute; Scott Klinger, United for a Fair Economy; Willian G. Gate and Peter R. Orszag, The Brookings Institute; Gary Bass, OMB Watch; Leonard Burman, Urban Institute; Rich Cohen, NCRP; Betty Ahrens, Iowa Citizen Action Network; Anita Dancs, National Priorities Project; Isaiah Poole, Institute for America's Future, Robert Reich, University of California; Dean Baker, Center for Economic and Policy Research; Jim Lehrer, Mara Liasson, NPR; David Wessel, Wall Street Journal; Marc Ash, Truthout; Patrick J. Buchanan, the American Cause; John McLaughlin, James Barnes, National Journal; Alexis Simendinger, National Journal Group; David Brock, Media Matters for America; Gloria Borger, CBS/US News; Katrina vandal Heuvel, the Nation; Gwen Ifill, Washington Week; Alexander Cockburn & Jeffrey St. Clair, Counter Punch; Chuck Collins, Responsible Wealth; Bob McIntyre, Citizens for Tax Justice; Robert Greenstein, Center on Budget and Policy Priorities; Mark Halperin, Time Magazine; Jonah Goldberg, National Review; Edmund L. Andrews, New York Times Company; Dan Balz, Washington Post; Charlie Savage, Boston Globe; George Stephanopoulas, ABC News; Kenneth Paulson, USA Today; Bill Keller, LA Times; Jack Z.

Smith, Ft. Worth Star-Telegram; Robert Bixby, Concord Coalition; Cheryl Hall, Dallas Morning News; Dennis Prager, Townhall; T.D. Coo Nguyen, Institute on Taxation and Economic Policy; Jeff Milchen, Reclaim Democracy, org.; Andrea Mitchell, NV-BC News; Karen Tumulty, Times Magazine; Steve Rendall, FAIR; Tom Brokaw, NBC News; Amy Goodman, Democracy Now; Michael Scherer, the Nation; Duane Parde, NTU; Kathleen Hall Jamieson, Annenberg Public Policy Center; Greg Mitchell, Editor and Publisher; John Walcott, McClatchy Newspapers; Michelle Cottle, The New Republic; Michelle Bernard, Independent Women's Forum; Scott McConnell, the American Conservative; Rick Stengel, Time Magazine; Don Feder, Boston Herald; Donna Brazile, Brazile & Associates; Mort Zuckerman, US News & World Report; Wolf Blitzer, Fox News; Brent Bozell III, Media Research Center; E.J. Dionne Jr., NPR; Michele Norris, NPR; Bob Drogin, LA Times; Bill Kristal, Weekly Standard; Byron York, American Spectator; Candy Crowley, CNN; Kim Genardo, WNCN – TV; Nina Easton, the Boston Globe; Judy Woodruff, WETA-TV; Brian Lehrer, WNYC Radio; Joe Conason, New York Observer; Matthew Rothschild, The Progressive; Cathy Madison, The Utne Reader; Charles Peters, Washington Monthly; Jeff Zeleny, New York Times; John Maggs, National Journal; Charles Green, National Journal; Ellen Miller, The Sunlight Foundation; Martin Baron, The Boston Globe; Michael Cooke, Chicago-Sun-Times, Pat Mitchell, PBS; Jane Mayer, the New Yorker; Jim Naureckas, FAIR; Dean Baker, CEPR; Bob Herbert, NY Times; Maureen Dowd, NY Times; Laura Flanders, Counterspin; Jim Hightower; David Corn, the Nation; Ben A. Franklin, Washington Spectator; William Whitworth, Altantic Monthly; Professor James Edward Maule, Villanova University School of law; Chris Field, Townhall Magazine; Walter E. William, George Mason University; Gerald Marzorati, New York Times; Ben Bradlee, Washington Post; Dean Baquet, NY Times; David Mark, the Politico; John Judis, The New Republic; Chris Wallace, Fox News; Clarence Page, Tribune Media Service; Monika H. Bauertain & Marcia D. Grienberger, Mother Jones Magazine; Michael Duffy, Time Magazine; Lawrence Mishel, EPI; Ryan Ellis, ATR; Clay Waters, Media Research Center; Brit Hume, Fox News; Norah O'Donnell, MSNBC; Joe Klein, Time; Howard Fineman, Newsweek; Keith Olberman, NBC; Eugene Robinson, Washington Post.

Of these about 300 people: I got no response—except for the following:

1. Book to Tony Blankley and Tucker Carlson were returned to me.

2. Twenty-one letters were returned to me: Charles Babington c/o Washington Post, Michael Martin, NPR; Isaiah Poole, Institute for American's Future; Editor of the Grand Rapid Press, Jim Hightower, David Moore, the Sunlight Foundation; Cynthia Tucker c/o Universal Press Syndicate; William Whitworth, Atlantic Monthly; Duane Parde, NTU; Charles Peters, Washington Monthly; Jim Naureckas, FAIR; Ben A. Franklin, Washington Spectator; Jane Mayer, the New Yorker; Charlie Savage c/o Boston Globe; Judy Woodruff c/o WETA-TV; Dennis Cauchon c/o USA Today; Mort Zuckerman c/o US News & World Report; Robert Novak, CNN Crossfire; Doyle McManus, LA Times; Martin Baron, the Boston Globe; Pat Mitchell c/o PBS.

3. I got a return letter from Mike Connelly, executive editor of the Herald-Tribune, Peter G. Peterson, senior chairman & co-founder of the Blackstone Group; Senator Dianne Feinstein, and Senator Joe Lieberman, he said: "Regrettably, due to the huge volume of mail that I receive, I am only able to research and address comments sent to me from Connecticut residents."

4. I also got a letter from Al Gore: dated 2/20/08. He said: he looked forward to reading my book

This is one version of my letter:

My name & address
Name of organization
Date _____

Dear (name of person),

I am sending you a copy of the FrontPage of my new website—TheTaxGuardian – to enlighten the public on tax issues. It shows the front and back cover of my book: *Why the Reagan and Bush Tax-Cuts are Unfair* (Second Edition). And it has important updates—at the end. Check it out: I exposed the federal budget deception, accused President Bush with misrepresentation, defended the Death Tax, showed the difference between McCain and Obama on taxes, etc.

If, my website and my books: contain truths, allegations, and revelations—that the public desire to know; then, it is the responsibility of the media—to tell them. It has failed to do that.

Walter F. Picca

Based on the sale of my book—to the end of November 2008—and the low number of people visiting my website: my advertising campaign—has had very little impact. There are two possible answers:

1. These over 300 people of the mass media—informed--believes the information is unworthy—to be made public.

2. It is a media blockade—because, they have opposite views—about taxes.

I believe the information in my book and website should be made public: the editors and journalists of the mass media--do not.

Posted 12/2/08

BUSH'S LEGACY

Bush said September 20, 2007, at a news conference: that the economy was strong and would remain so if Congress steered clear of tax increases. Well, there has been no tax increases and the economy has turned sour.

And he said: "You need to talk to economists. I think I got a B in Econ 101. I got an A, however, in keeping taxes low."

Bush is a truth twister: the first huge tax cut that he pushed through congress: the Economic Growth and Tax Relief Act of 2001: he said at the signing was tax relief for "hard working Americans"; like, Steven and Josefina Ramos, who had a little girl, here with us. But, the truth of the matter: 50 percent of the tax relief will go to the top 1 percent by 2011.

The second huge tax cut that he pushed through congress: the Jobs and Growth Tax Relief Reconciliation Act of 2003: he said at the signing "we are helping workers who need more take-home pay." This time he used David and Jenny Theison, as an example, who worked hard for their children.

Bush said: "under the bill I sign, it's going to be a lot easier for the Theison family…." Here again: emphasizing: it is a tax cut for hard working people, when, in fact, it contains super-big tax cuts for the rich, like himself, the vice-president, his cabinet—and corporate executives—who receive dividends and capital gains. That part was missing in his bill signing remarks.

He said—you need to talk to economists: let's do that. Here is what Noble economist, Joseph Stiglitz said: "The first major economic initiative by the president was a massive tax cut for the rich, enacted in June of 2001. Those with incomes over a million got a tax cut of $18,000—more than 30 times larger than the cut received by the average American. The inequities were compounded by a second tax cut, in 2003, this one skewed even more heavily toward the rich."

Therefore, Bush deserves A for cutting taxes on the wealthy, but, he deserves F for raising the National Debt. This part—he never mentions.

The estimated deficit for 2008: $455 billion. That figure is partial. It does not include off-budget expenses.

For seven years, he ignored the facts: that the national debt was growing faster--than economic growth. By the time Bush leaves office: he will add close to $5 trillion to the National Debt. That is nearly double—and a heavy drag on the economy: the interest and principle payments. The interest for fiscal year 2008: $451 billion, for which the taxpayers get nothing. The estimated budget deficit for 2009--over $1 trillion.

Ten Noble laureates and 450 economists voiced opposition to the $750 billion, ten year tax cuts--that he proposed in 2003. Here is part of their statement:

"The tax cut plan proposed by President Bush is not the answer to the problems."

"Passing these tax cuts will worsen the long-term budget outlook, adding to the Nation's projected chronic deficits."

"Moreover, the proposed tax cuts will generate further inequalities in after-tax income."

George Akerlof, Nobel economist, who also signed the statement opposing the Bush tax cuts, said:

"It's a horrendous bill."

"It seeks to redistribute wealth in the wrong direction, in a very big way, to the very wealthiest end of the spectrum."

"My answer is that the tax cuts will decrease revenues, resulting in deficits."

Noble economist, Joseph Stiglitz told the BBC's World Business Report that Mr. Bush's plans were "fiscal madness, fiscal irresponsibility."

Noble economist, Modigliani, who also signed the statement said: "This tax proposal of the President is bad."

The final version of the bill was pared down to $350 billion: extending some tax cuts for eight years. It passed the House and the Senate with vice-president Cheney casting the tie breaker vote—despite the signed statement by the hundreds of economists --because, of greed—and republicans had the power in congress—and used phony supply-side economic arguments to justify it—also called: trickle down economics.

Bush ignored his own chief economic adviser, Gregory Mankiw, who wrote in his macroeconomic textbooks that there is "no credible evidence" that tax cuts pay for themselves, and that an economist who makes such a claim is a "snake oil salesmen who is trying to sell a miracle cure."

In August of 2004: after two Bush tax cuts were enacted: ten noble economists signed a letter supporting John Kerry for president—stating: "President Bush and his administration have embarked on a reckless and extreme course that endangers the long-term economic health of our nation...."

That proved to be correct.

Noble economist: Joseph Stiglitz, who also signed the letter said: "Here, as elsewhere, Bush is dead wrong, and too dogmatic to admit it."

And he said: the US tax code has become: "hideously biased in favor of the rich."

When, Bush made this statement in September 2007, that economy was strong: he was trying to put a good face on the economy; when, it fact: it was in trouble: he was living in La-La Land.

He was ignoring the slowing economy: growth in the first three quarters was the lowest since 2002.

He was ignoring the subprime mortgage crisis—the increase in the number of home foreclosures in 2007.

He was ignoring the soaring National Debt.

Now, did his tax cuts grow the economy?—yes, a little; but, it was more economic growth from credit expansion: private and government. It was temporary (or illusory)—from not paying bills.

Did his tax cuts create jobs: a little, temporarily, but, not long-term. The unemployment rate—now--is the highest in 14 years. The government reported--employers cut 240,000 jobs in October.

Did the Bush tax cuts help workers take home more pay: House Budget Committed reported in July, 2008: Real median household income has decreased almost $1,000 under Bush:

I give Bush a D for econ 101.

But since, Bush introduced the Ramos and Thieson family at the signing of his two tax cut economic growth bills: I believe it is fitting—to revisit them—to see how they are doing...Are they better off?

Bush spoke to soon, when he said; he deserves a B for Econ 101. The economy—presently, is in an economic downturn. "It's pretty clear that we're in a recession," said Robert Brusca, economist at FAO Economics. Job loss in 2008 to November: 1.2 million.

It is official: the National Bureau of Economic Research said (Monday): its group of academic economists met and decided: The US economy has been in a recession since December 2007.

FOUR LETTERS

12/7/08
Dear Mr. Warren Buffett,

I have posted an article on my blog—thetaxguardian.com, dated 11/8/08--about you "the Oracle of Omaha": would you check it out—and give me your reaction. You could help enlighten America.

I will post your answer on my blog.

Walter F. Picca

12/7/08

Dear Mr. Al Gore,

Thank you for your letter. However, I must ask more from you. You said, you were going to read my book. I want you opinion. I gave you my opinion—about your book.

Also—check out my blog: thetaxguardian.com. Do you think—this information is good (or bad) for the American people. I think—a debate by experts on Current TV—about the tax principles that I have put forth--would be useful. You are the co-founded and an expert on these matters…and I will post your remarks on my blog. Democracy—depends on informed people.

The problem—I have run into a media blockade. I have given two possible reasons on my blog—which do you think it is?

American values your opinion.

Walter F. Picca

12/7/08

Dear Mr. Ross Perot,

I posted an article about you: "Ross Perot, the Boss" dated 8/5/08 on my blog: thetaxguardian.

com. Could you give me your reaction? Do you agree or disagree? Your billions and opinion is valuable to the American people. I believe—I am carrying out the work—you stated—reducing US National Debt. However, I have run into a media blockade.

I will post your answer on my blog.

Walter F. Picca

12/7/08

Dear Mr. Peter G. Peterson,

First, thank you for your letter. Remember: I sent you my book: *Why the Reagan and Bush Tax-cuts are Unfair.* However, I was not satisfied with your comment; I want your opinion—or review. Recently, I read you book: *Running on Empty*—which I agree with: **Bush's tax cuts have squandered an era of prosperity and doomed our kids to a crippled economy....** I heard you say on the Charlie Rose show: you made more money than you know what to do with. I know what to do with it. Aside from that, give your comments—whether the information in my book and on my blog: thetaxguardian—is correct or good for the American people. It needs a jolt.

I will post your answer on my blog.

Walter F. Picca

Posted 12/10/08

OBAMA—THE PANDERER, THE FOOL, THE IDIOT...

(revised)

Obama said on television the night before the election: he was going to give the middle class a tax cut—and senior citizens with income less than $50,000 would not pay income tax under his plan. He also ran an ad stating: his middle class tax cut was three times bigger than McCain's: that is conning the public to get votes. He is not the candidate of change.

A true man would not mislead the voters. The economic situation has changed—since—he first began campaigning. His tax proposals are obsolete. He put himself in straightjacket.

If, he continues to pursue the same tax proposals outlined earlier in his campaign: he will rack up off-the-charts federal deficits. Paulson recently said: "I will never apologize for changing a strategy or an approach if the facts change."

The facts have change—but, Obama has not.

The facts changed—when he voted: YEA on the $700 billion bailout of Wall Street, that was laden with an additional $120 billion in pork and tax-breaks for the upper class. The income tax deductions in this bill are greater than the median family income of $50,233. It was passed by bribing members of congress. By voting for that bill: he must admit: his middle class tax cut, his $500 tax credit, etc. are no longer prudent. In fact, they were never prudent. He is a white-black panderer: he rather win the election—than tell the truth. He should have told the American people—the truth prior to election day.

The estimated deficit for 2009—more than $1 trillion; yet, he continues to promise tax cuts: he is dishonest. He said: he will always tell the American people the truth. The truth is—his tax cuts are irresponsible.

He also recently said: "I will outlaw torture." You mean to say; if, the terrorist attack--that happened in Mumbai, India—killing 172 and wounding 295, plus property damage--happened here—and a terrorist was captured alive: he would not use harsh interrogation techniques—to get information about their secret operation, its source, etc. He is a damn fool.

There is a difference—between torture of the good—opposed to the torture of the evil—to save lives. The good are opposed to evil and the evil are opposed to good. Some says: it doesn't work—that is probably because—they are using the wrong method—some used at Gitmo.

It does work—there are cases. If, what you did is wrong—it is wrong—to conceal the people or group behind it.

Terrorists— blow up buildings, injuring and killing innocent people, they set off car bombs in crowded streets, throw acid in the face of girls, who attend school; they kill aid workers and journalists, they plant bombs in roadways, they are planning attacks—where they can kill the most people.

I heard a Cabad house chairman on a TV news program say-- to mourners of a couple slain in Mumbai—of those terrorists: "May they burn in hell." I would go further than that: I believe they should burn on earth—be tortured—if, they refuse to talk. You cannot root out terrorism—unless you know the source. Those that commit these heinous acts—know the source. I believe: the torture of a guilty terrorist—is justified—to get the information—to save the life of one innocent person.

Barack Hussein Obama does not. He said, "I have never made an exception for torture and I never will."

He would not use torture—to get information to capture (or kill) Osama bin Laden, which he says "is critical."

He would not use torture—pain—to get information: to prevent a chemical, biological, or nuclear attack on American.

He would not use torture—to prevent 9/11.

He—might not be so sympathetic with terrorists—if, was his wife and daughters were killed—or maimed in an attack.

Terrorists are not the same as POWs.

I have outlined—when torture is justified—in my book: "Why the Reagan and Bush tax-cuts are unfair (second edition).

He should read it. He is a benevolent idiot! He feels more for the terrorists—than the victims. He should log on to: facethefire.org. He suffered second and third degree burns over 60 percent of his body from a terrorist attack. Torture—or harsh interrogation techniques should be retained—as an optional weapon against terrorism, the same as the atomic bomb against aggression, the same as the death penalty—against violent crime. However, torture may not be necessary, if, one follows the right protocol. I also noticed: he has a slight swagger—when he goes to the podium. Actually, he is not as smart—as he thinks he is. America has elected a semi-moron for president.

Obama said: "We need a Commander in Chief who has never wavered on whether or not it is acceptable for America to torture, because it is never acceptable." He is wrong. India names Pakistani masterminds only days after the Mumbai attack. They got some of it from the surviving gunman. The head of the crime branch said: "A terrorist of this sort is never cooperative. We have to extract information." Indian police use interrogation methods that are regarded as torture to the West. Obama would have read the captured terrorist—his Miranda rights. Because, he says: torture is never acceptable—and the captured gunman would have remained silent without the threat of torture—or its use.

Tim Vaculik says:

"Morons! When will you come to understanding that the enemy must be Dealt With in whatever terms required to protect and defend our country." This man is more right than the president-elect. It is not immoral to use torture—on a recalcitrant perpetrator--to bring to justice those responsible and prevent future such attacks. It is immoral not to do so—unless, he thinks these terrorists are right. He is headed for a clobbering…some of his agenda is flawed.

Ruling out torture—100 percent—would put America in handcuffs—against the most diabolical terrorists—the world has even seen.

PRESIDENT BUSH--THE SINGLE BIGGEST WASTER OF TAXPAYER DOLLARS— AND ACCOMPLISHES—VERY LITTLE... EXCEPT—BIG PUBLIC DEBT.

Recently, lawmakers blasted auto executives for flying to Capital Hill—in corporate or private jets—to ask for a bailout; but—what about Bush, the U.S. President.

I speaking of Air Force One—or the Flying White House—when Bush travels: it is on a 747—that burns 4,000 gallons fuel and cost $56,800 to operate per hour—plus two huge cargo planes—carrying his armored limousine, a backup limo, an ambulance, sometimes his helicopter, etc. In addition: his aides, secret agents, and other support. The total cost is classified.

I believe Bush is abusing that perk:

1. He campaigns—back and forth across the country—in Air Force One—and reimbursing the government only—with the cost of 1st class commercial air fare for himself and aides. That is a big advantage over—other candidates—that pay for their jet used in campaigning. To make this more fair: he should pay what it would cost, if he had to charter and operate a jet—the same as his rival.

2. Reported May 31, he traveled to 24 fund raisers on Air Force One in 2004, that is political—not official government business. He reimburses the government— only the cost of commercial first class airfare for himself and aides. It is not cost effective—either for his party—or the people. Secondly, it uses taxpayer money to subsidize his choice—not necessarily the people's. Therefore, Air Force One should not be used for political fund raisers.

3. He flew to his ranch in Crawford, Texas on Air Force One—for vacations 77 times up to September 2007. He has spent close to 826 days on vacation during his two terms in office: beating Reagan's record of 335 days. That is clearly excessive—vacation time should be limited. He spends so much time on vacation: Source Watch calls Bush: "the War President missing in action."

4. The second place he flies for vacations is to Kennebunkport, Maine, where he has a summer home—on Air Force One.

I believe the total cost of these flights should be made public—so, we can put a stop to this extravagance—or waste of taxpayer money. I think the people are going to be appalled; when—they hear: the total cost to fly Bush on Air Force One around the world on official business, for campaign appearances, for political fund raisers, back and forth from Washington DC—to Crawford, Texas—and Kennebunkport, Maine—on vacations. It has gotten—out of control!

It started in a C-54 used by president Roosevelt, Truman used a DC-6, Eisenhower—traveled on a Lockheed C-121, Nixon used a VC-25 and a Boeing 707 jet, Kennedy upgraded to a C-137 Stratoliner, Reagan ordered two 747s, Bush uses two 747s, and two C-5 Galaxy heavy aircraft to transport his limousines, helicopter, and other equipment. He also has a fleet of 18 helicopters. It goes on and on. Recently, the Pentagon ordered 28 new super-sophisticated helicopters to serve as Marine One: costing: $11.2 billion.

Bush spent 27 percent of his time as president on vacation—compared to 5.7 percent for Clinton. That is taking advantage of taxpayers. He cut more than 150 government programs—to reduce the deficits, but his official, political and private vacation travels costs were greatly increased—compared to other presidents. And, the benefits of his US and world travel—on Air Force One—not much—or negative. Bush breaks the record for days spent on vacation and miles logged on Air Force One—but, he won't state number or cost. It is our money —we have a right to know!

I don't know who is worst—President Bush or King Abdullah.

Posted 12/27/08

THE BUDGET DEFICIT IN CALIFORNIA AND NEW YORK ARE SIMILAR (I.E., THE PROBLEM).

In California—it is partly Governor Schwarzenegger: he has a Hummer ego and a Studebaker mind. He said: at a news conference—in his defense: He does not represent a party, he represents the people. That is false: he endorsed McCain for president: that is representing his party—not the people.

The budget deal signed in September—is already outdated. The deepening recession has increased the revenue shortfall—to $42 billion by mid 2010.

On 12/22, Schwarzenegger held a news conference at Westwood, where he blamed the halt in a freeway construction project on the legislature inaction. The real: culprit: his repeal of the Gray Davis car-tax.

Actually, the day prior to the Westwood news conference, the legislature did pass an $18 billion package of cuts and new revenues. But, he has threatened to veto it—because, he said: it is not a real budget solution.

But, that is not possible without tax increases.

The real obstruction: every republican member of the legislature except one, has signed a pledge vowing never to increase taxes. That puts democrats in a squeeze. There are two legitimate means of ending a budget deficit: increase taxes and cutting expenses. Republicans—have renounced half of their power to fix the budget—to block higher taxes, principally, on the wealthy. That is wrong. Tax increases, sometimes, are justified. I believe—taking a no tax increase pledge—should be illegal—or denounced.

Republicans are able to block essential tax increases—because, it takes a 2/3rds majority to raise taxes in California. Until that law is changed: the repeat budget crisis will continue.

The governor wants the legislature to cut government expenses, which requires laying off state workers--and at the same time—increase outlays for infrastructure projects: to promote job growth. That is a contradiction. It does not make sense to lay off people to cut government expenses and at the same time increase government outlays—to promote job growth.

If, republicans block tax increases: that leaves democrats with the only other major solution: cut government expenses.

The democrats have made $7.2 billion in cuts: in public schools, corrections, California and state universities, local public safety programs, money for needy and disabled, public transit, and welfare cost-of-living increases, etc.—on top of the $11 billion in September. The Republicans have not agreed to any corresponding tax increases. No republicans voted for the budget deal.

The LA Times reported: the governor complained: that the recently passed budget package--did not include an additional $1.5 billion in cuts to the state workforce and welfare programs.

There is a point: where you cannot cut expenses more without doing harm to the state of California: cutting essential services, medical care for the unfortunate, raising college intuition, increasing unemployment, etc.

The governor budget proposals--required layoffs to cut cost, and then he criticizes the democrats for passing a budget plan—that does not do enough to promote job growth. He is nuts.

And, republicans refuse to budge!

New York State has a similar problem: Its governor, David Paterson, is legally blind—and it has a $15.4 billion budget deficit.

First of all, I believe seeing is required to govern a state--and the law should bar the legally blind from holding offices of leadership. Would you give a legally blind person a driver's license? No.

The governor of a state—should be able to read the bills he signs and act wisely in an emergency: Paterson is unable to do that. And, he is off the tracks on a number of issues, particularly, taxes.

The Bill Moyers interview—shows: he has mental impairment. He wants to tax music downloads on the Internet, haircuts, movie tickets, taxis rides, sporting events, and extends the sales tax to cable and satellite TV services, etc. Probably, his most bizarre tax increase—is on sodas—to prevent obesity. I can think of a better one than that: reduce food stamps to the overweight and obese. He says: "What I am afraid of is taxing the wealthy now, which in New York we're fond of doing, still having a deficit, where are we going to go then? Tax the wealthy again? No." He is wrong. New York has cut the top income tax more than 50 percent since 1972. And, since the income of the top 1 percent—has dramatically increased—since then: higher rates are justified. Taxing a worker's income from $20,000 to $40,000 and a Wall Street executive's bonus of $5 million—the same: is not fair. First—you raise taxes on the most able to pay—then—the less.

To close the budget gap, he has—proposed 153 fee and tax increases: to fix the revenue shortfall: that hits the low income earners the most, to a lesser degree the middle class, and no pain for the rich. That is wrong. New York has the second highest state and local taxes—of the nation.

New York state also has a heavy concentration of wealth: 74 of the 400 wealthiest Americans live in New York State: ranging from $1.3 to $20 billion. It is the home for 10.5 percent of all Americans earning more than $200,000. In 2006, the top 1 percent had three times the income of the bottom 50 percent. They can afford to pay more taxes.

The NY state income tax hits the working man the hardest: 6.85 percent over $20,000. After, $20,000 there is no higher bracket—or tax rate. Governor Paterson says: he finds taxing the wealthy—unappealing. He is wrong. I agree with Jonathan Tasini, he said:

"We could wipe out the budget deficit—or, certainly trim it down to something trivial—by raising taxes on the very wealthy and going back to a more progressive taxation system that we had in the 1970s. You know this: if the state replaced the existing rate structure (consisting of 5 brackets with rates ranging from 4.0 to 6.85%) with one consisting of 14 brackets with rates ranging from 2.0 to 15.0%, we could bring in $6-7 billion more, and perhaps as high as $11 billion."

Those that benefit the most—by living in a state—should pay a higher percentage tax: that is correct. Executives working on Wall Street are not going to move to a different state—where there are no bonuses.

Under a plan advanced by the labor-backed Working Families Party: marginal income between $500,000 and $1 million would be taxed at a rate of 9.35%, between $1 million and $5 million….10.35%, between $5 million and $10 million…11.85%, and income above $10 million would be taxed at 13.85 %. That would make the New York state income tax a lot fairer.

Senate Republicans have said they would oppose increasing the personal income tax. That is the same problem in California. That leaves taxing the lower and middle class—as the only alternative (i.e., to raising revenues)—and cutting government expenses and laying off more state workers during a recession. Dean G. Skelos, the Senate majority leader and Long Island Republican said: "We simply cannot raise taxes when our economy is struggling." New Yorkers earning over $100,000 per year—are not struggling. The income of the top 1 percent of New Yorkers has risen 232 percent from 1976 to 2006--and their income tax cut more than 50 percent. Right now, the NY income tax on incomes to $30,000 is too high and the tax on incomes over $80,000 is too low. It needs to revamp its income tax tables.

Let's see what happens!

Posted 12/29/08

FIFTH LETTER

I sent this letter to Michael R. Bloomberg, New York City Mayor, and fourth richest New Yorker: worth $11.5 billion

12/29/09
Dear Mayor Michael Bloomberg,

I would like your opinion on an article I posted on my blog: thetaxguardian.com – on 12/27/08—about the New York State deficit, particularly, do you support higher income taxes on the wealthy?

Walter F. Picca

IS BUSH—A LIAR, A DECEIVER, JUST WRONG—OR ALL THREE?

(revised)

He accused Al Gore in his first presidential debate of "phony numbers"; when, he said: "he (Bush) will spend more money on tax cuts for the wealthiest 1%, than all of the new spending that he proposes for education, healthcare, prescription drugs, and national defense combined."

Al Gore was correct.

In the second debate, Bush said: the top 1% would receive less in tax cuts—than the figure stated by Gore. He was wrong again: he left out the cost of the estate tax cuts and repeal—in his computation.

Bush continued to misstate facts during his two terms in office—including the Iraq lies, manipulation of evidence—or bad intelligence. Bush says: it was bad intelligence. I have my own opinion, but this is not the focus of this blog. It is taxes and related matters.

Seven years in a row, he hoodwinked the American people—by reporting a partial federal spending deficit. It did not include off-budget expenses. He used the phony deficit—to claim his tax cuts were working. He did not count the billions siphoned from the Social Security Trust Fund, etc.

He pledged to put the Social Security paid-in-surplus in a lockbox—he did not: he siphoned it off—to pay for the Afghanistan and Iraq wars, etc.

Bush—never—mentioned in his State of Union Addresses: the total yearly deficits his administration—added to the National Debt.

He cited gains and ignored losses.

He deceived—the American people—by emphasizing his tax cuts were for the benefit of workers, families, and small businesses; when, the top 20% got 74% and the bottom 80% got 26%.

The biggest miscalculation of all: the Bush administration projected in 2001: a $4.5 trillion surplus—over the next ten years. That was more than a $10 trillion error. By the end of 2008—almost $5 trillion was added to the National Debt. That is almost double—in eight years.

Here are some of his errors—or distortions in his annual budget message to the Congress:

For FY 2001: "To make sure the retirement savings of the American's seniors are not diverted into other programs, my budget protects all $2.6 trillion of Social Security for Social Security and for Social Security alone."

And, he further stated: there was a fork in the road—one would dip into Social Security: the wrong road. However, the entire paid in surplus up to 2001—has already been spent—and he spent the entire paid in surplus for the next eight years. At the end of his two terms: there was zero money in the Trust Fund.

And he said, "It's not fair to tax the same earnings twice—once when you earn them, and again when you die—so we must repeal the death tax". This shows his goal—right from the start.

There are a number of things wrong with this statement: it is fair—if, you paid too little taxes—and left a federal debt. It is fairer to tax—the deceased—for this debt--than the new born.

According to one study: estates worth over $10 million are made up of 56.4% untaxed capital gains. This does not include estates of billionaires. So, this double taxation argument is seriously flawed. It is not double taxation from a different perspective: the increase in the national debt during the life of the decedent—means he/she was under taxed. Therefore, the estate tax collects taxes owed from the estate of the decedent—before it is transferred to the next generation.

The US tax code recognizes private debt—it does not recognize public debt: that is a big fatal defect—or loophole.

Without a death (or inheritance) tax—workers will not only have to pay off the government debts of the previous generation, as well as, support a class of people who live off of inherited wealth—to a large degree from capital gains, that has never been taxed. Harvard did a bad job…educating Bush Jr.

For FY 2002, he said: "This budget offers a new vision for governing our Nation." It would reduce the debt by $2 trillion over 10 years. It increased the debt: $5 trillion in eight years--instead. Bush reminds us, that in 2001—he provided a typical family of four: $1,600 in tax relief. The reason, he said: Americans have been overcharged for Government. You know that is false; since, 1980—or Reagan: the National Debt has increased every year—except one. The Clinton surpluses were achieved, in part, by spending the S.S. paid-in-surpluses off-budget. That debt was not included in the budget deficit. There was no surplus in 2001—when you add the off-budget expense. Bush was deceitful or dumb.

For FY 2003, he said: "The 2003 Budget requests the biggest increase in defense spending in twenty years, to pay the cost of war…." But, there is no request for a tax increase to pay for it. In fact, his budget plan calls for: maintaining low tax rates (i.e., mostly on the rich). He failed to mention: the 2002 total federal deficit was $317 billion.

For FY 2004, he said: "And for America's 84 million investors and those who will become investors, I propose eliminating the double taxation of stock dividends. Double taxation us unfair and bad for the economy."

The first sentence is a distortion: 84 million investors, own stocks, but not all dividend paying stocks. Dividend paying stocks are owned mostly by the rich—or big investors: 65% of dividends go to the top 5%.

He is also wrong double taxation is not unfair—because, not all corporations pay income (or profit) taxes—or pay far less than the statutory rate. Double taxation can be fair; e.g., the federal and state income taxes. It becomes unfair—when the combined rate is excessive. It is not.

Taxing dividends paid to shareholders is not bad for the economy—unless all forms of taxation are bad. They are necessary. He failed to mention: there was a total federal deficit in 2003 of $536 billion.

For FY 2005, he said: "With this spending restraint and continued pro-growth economic polices, we can cut the deficit in half over the next five years." What deficit is he talking about—the budget or total federal deficit which includes off-budget expenses, which he never mentions. The total federal deficit for 2004: $567 billion

For FY 2006, he said: "We are launching innovative programs such as Cover the Kids, which will expand health insurance coverage for needy children." In October 2007, he vetoed the Child Health Care Bill.

He also said: "I look forward to working closely with Congress to achieve these reductions and reforms. By doing so, we will remain on track to meet our goal to cut the deficit in half by 2009." Well, this is 2009 and the estimated deficit—over $1.75 trillion: triple the 2004 deficit.

For FY 2007, he said: "Since, May 2003, when I signed into law major tax relief …" Here, he is admitting to a grave mistake. The signing took place May 28, after the Iraq invasion or war started. This was a good reason to raise taxes—not cut taxes on the richest Americans. Later in 2007, top Democrats proposed a war surtax—in response to Bush's request for money. Rep. Dave Obey (D-WI), who co-sponsored the bill, said the surtax is a way for "this generation" to pay for the Iraq War. The plan was quickly condemned by Republicans.

Bush further stated in his budget message: "In our efforts to keep our economy strong and competitive, we will resist calls to raise taxes on America's workers, families, and businesses." But, it was not this group—that got the biggest share of his tax cuts. It was people like himself—the top 2 percent, which he never mentions. What he really meant: we will resist calls to repeal his tax cuts; mostly on the rich, which he did. Any ways, it did not keep the economy strong. He failed to mention the total deficit for 2006: $602 billion.

For FY 2008, he said: "The Federal deficit is declining and on a path to elimination. Last year, we successfully met our goal of cutting the deficit in half, three years ahead of schedule." What the hell deficit is he talking about: the National Debt, which has skyrocketed in the last seven years—or the partial budget deficit—which excludes off-budget expenses (i.e., the Iraq War)? The Federal deficit Bush was referring to—was the partial $244 billion budget deficit--according to the World Almanac: the total federal deficit for 2007: $521 billion. So, he is misstating the facts again.

For FY 2009, he said: "As we enter this New Year, our economy retains a solid foundation despite some challenges, revenues have reached record levels, and we have reduced the Federal deficit by $250 billion since 2004." Here, Bush is delusional. He gave this message to Congress, in February of 2008—after the recession began. The foundation is crumbling, the cost of the wars in Iraq and Afghanistan is mounting, and revenues were far short of meeting government expenses. The total Federal deficit for 2008: $985 billion—a U.S. record.

He claims: our economy has grown for six years: yes it did—modestly, but, federal debt grew faster. The reason it grew: taxes were cut, mostly on the rich, not paying for government expenses, lowering credit and lending standards, turning a blind eye to signs of trouble in the housing market, over borrowing: private and public—until the economy collapsed—in 2008. Private debt grew faster than income. Government debt grew faster than revenues. It was economic growth—based on the imprudent expansion of credit and rising house and stock prices—or flatulence--more than tangible or real. Bush also never mentioned trade deficits—in any of his annual congressional budget messages. He painted a false picture of the economy for eight years.

The Center for American Progress states: Bush's Tax and Budget Polices Fail to Promote Economic Growth.

Bush continues to shade the truth—or deny the facts—to the very end. He said in his final press conference: "You know, it's kind of like, Why me? Oh, the burdens, you know. Why did the financial collapse have to happen on my watch? It's just – it's pathetic, isn't it, self pity."

Here, he is denying responsibility—like, it was an earthquake—something that just happened—beyond human control and he is a victim.

The reason it happened: his pro-growth (bad) policies.

Posted: 1/31/09

BUSH'S FINAL TALLY

(revised)

Bush said in his 2007 State of the Union address: we can balance the budget without a tax increase: that is—clearly--not realistic.

This is the Bush deficit deception. The Bush administration official budget deficits from 2002—to the end of fiscal 2008: total $2.2 trillion: the total increase in the National

Debt for the same period: $4.3 trillion: the difference between the two: $2.1 trillion spent (or borrowed) off-budget—which the US government—has never given an account for. By leaving government expenses off budget, Bush makes us think—his tax cuts are responsible for lower budget deficits. When, in fact, you add the off-budget expenses: they are responsible for increasing the National Debt.

The people—should demand that the U.S. government tell us—what the off-budget expenses are. We have a right to know--it is our money. The only justification for not including government expenses in the budget—they were not foreseeable—when the budget was made, such as: Katrina, the start of wars, etc. During the Bush administration, there has been a $2.1 trillion increase in debt—that is not budget deficits. And the American people have been to busy watching sports and x-rated moves—to inquire for what—and the mass media has not told them. Why, they are the big beneficiaries. The Bush tax cuts; mostly, on the wealthy were totally irresponsible and irresponsible and immoral for not increasing them during the Afghanistan and Iraq Wars—or seven years of deficits.

When, I see the photo of Bush signing the $350 billion tax cuts: May 28, 2003--after the commencement of the Iraq War--and the four men smiling behind him—I see in them: Hitler and his top aides planning the looting of Europe. Goering said, his collection of art was legal—when, in fact--it was plunder. It is the same principle: the setting is different. It is the principle of absolute power over ruling the law—or making the law: Republicans controlled the congress.

The different between the national debt when Bush took office and it ended; nearly, $5 trillion: Bush used his office to steal—legally.

Here is how Senator Patty Murray describes his tax cut: "Today, amid great fanfare, the President signed another tax cut to benefit a few".…."a record increase in America's debt".…."the government is borrowing another $350 billion to give away in tax cuts, mostly to the elite".…."these tax cuts force cuts in other important priorities".…."state governments are being force to increase states taxes to cover state shortfalls".…."we are now borrowing money from our children in order to finance tax cuts for the wealthy" and she said: "I hope that as the President touts his latest tax cut, he will remember the costs of his actions – to other priorities today and to our children tomorrow."

Bush sees it differently, he said July 11, 2006: "Together, these tax cuts left nearly $1.1 trillion in the hands of American workers and families and small–business owners." He fails to mention these tax cuts added to the National Debt—it is like: he gave you $10 in tax cuts—and put $15 on your credit card.

He misrepresented the tax cuts: the CBO states: millionaires got a larger share of the tax cuts than the bottom 80 percent. Bush always refers to American workers and families and small-business owners as the beneficiaries of his tax cuts—never, the top 2 percent—who got the bigger share.

Bush claims his tax cuts; mostly on the rich—have lowered the budget deficit. He does not tell us—he is siphoning money from the Social Security and Medicare Trust Funds—to pay for off-budget expenses--increasing the National Debt. That, he never mentions in his State of Union Addresses. That is deception.

The government has two sets of books: it shows us one and hides the other: that is fraud. There is no place—you can get the facts.

Bush said in the 2009 budget address to congress: "To help Americans see where their money is being spent, we have launched a website called: www.USAspending.gov...." But, nowhere can I find on that website—what the Social Security and Medicare paid-in-surplus was spent on—for the last eight years—or what the off-budget expenses are—or the consistency of the different between budget deficits and the increase of the National Debt for each fiscal year. It is restricted to government contracts, grants, loans, etc. It does not chart the destination of earmarks or TARP money—either.

Bush's two failed robbery attempts of the US government: the elimination of the dividend and estate tax—both fair and essential sources of revenues: both tax cuts; highly, favor the superrich.

Here are the costs of his actions:

- In 2008: economic growth slowed, and declined 0.5% in the 3Q and 3.8% in the 4Q: the biggest—since 1982.

- In 2008: 533,000 jobs were lost in November, 524,000 in December: that brings the total: to 2.6 million for 2008.

- In 2008: 1.06 million consumer bankruptcies were filed—up 33% from 2007.

- In 2008: 50 million families cannot pay off their credit card debt.

- In 2008: one out of ten homeowners cannot pay their mortgages or are in foreclosure.

- Wall Streets ends it worst year—since 1931.

- From Jan. 20 of 2001 to Jan. 20 of 2009: Bush added to the National debt—nearly $5 trillion: that is almost as much as all presidents preceding him.

- During the Bush administration: the GDP grew 45 percent: national debt grew almost 100 percent: his tax cuts to grow the economy, create jobs, and reduce the National Debt are an abysmal failure.

- Bush told ABC's Charles Gibson: "I leave the presidency with my head up high"; apparently, he is not looking at the economy.

- In late 2008, the US government has loaned, invested, or committed an additional $7.8 trillion to rescue—the economy from its tailspin: $200 billion for Freddie Mac and Fannie Mae, $29 billion for Bear Stearns, $150 billion for AIG, $350 billion for Citigroup, $300 billion for FHA, $500 billion to rescue various credit markets, $87 billion for JP Morgan Chase, trillions for the FDIC, etc.

- As of January 19, 2009: the National debt has soared to $10.64 trillion and growing at the rate of $3.4 billion per day.

- The interest on the National Debt for FY 2008: $451 billion—the third largest expense of the budget. That is the folly of increased spending (i.e., for two wars)--and cutting taxes, mostly on the rich: the Bush pro-growth economic polices. He continues to believe he is right—despite the Tsunami of evidence against him. He began office with a budget surplus, tax rebates, and tax cuts, mostly on the elite—and ended with a U.S. record budget deficit, rising job losses, and a deepening recession.

"This downturn promises to be the worst since the Great Depression in the 1930s, said Joshua Shapiro, chief US economist at the forecasting firm MTR Inc.

"We've only just started. I can't see bottoming out until sometime in 2010."

FOR LATER POSTINGS:
See my blog: www.thetaxguardian.com